Just Want to be Loved for Me...

Bev Thomas-Graham

authorHOUSE

AuthorHouse™ UK Ltd.
500 Avebury Boulevard
Central Milton Keynes, MK9 2BE
www.authorhouse.co.uk
Phone: 08001974150

©2010 Bev Thomas-Graham. All rights reserved.

No part of this book may be reproduced, stored in a retrieval system, or transmitted by any means without the written permission of the author.

First published by AuthorHouse 10/1/2010

ISBN: 978-1-4520-4649-5 (sc)

This book is printed on acid-free paper.

Dedication

I dedicate this book to my children Richie, Shanaz and Josh in recognition of their support and patience during the many hours taken up in preparing this work.

I also dedicate this to my sisters: Norma Juggan, Edna Thomas, Valerie Pitt, Elreta Brown, Joyce Hanson and Ruby Williams.

Last but not least, I dedicate this book to my little sister Denise Williams, whose tireless efforts in supporting me through the writing and editing process proved invaluable.

Finally, this book is for all of my spiritual sisters, especially those who are strong women of God. They have taught me the true meaning of 'Girl Power' in modern times, and the importance of being all you can be as you walk with God !

Thank you...

To my husband Billy Graham for his endless love, support and belief in me which helped me to finally undertake the process to get this book out to the readers.

P.S.
No, he is not 'THE' Billy Graham - the TV evangelist... (I did hear you wondering...) but he is also a strong man of God, prophetically called after his namesake into ministry. You will always be **'THE'** Billy Graham for me.

Love you always. B. xx

Acknowledgments

Firstly, I give honour to my heavenly Father for his grace and mercy in my life, and also for choosing me to be used as a vessel of his love. I also recognise and thank him for the support and guidance of the Holy Spirit in writing this book, often late at night and into the early hours of the quiet morning. So often when I was bereft of the ability to sleep after tossing and turning restlessly, I was only able to find peaceful rest after giving in and getting up to write, thus submitting in obedience to his voice.

My heartfelt gratitude and thanks go to my church family, 'The Tabernacle' in Lewisham, South London. In particular, I want to thank the man of vision himself, Senior Pastor Michael White and his team for providing the leadership and fertile spiritual ground for me to be nurtured and developed in.

I also acknowledge and thank Apostle Caleb and First Lady Yvonne Mackintosh for their patience, guidance and support over the years. They acted in complete obedience to the voice of God and had faith in me in spite of my lack of official titles and training. This opened the doors that allowed me to teach Theology at the Bibleway Training

Institute in London. It also allowed me to teach and present to their related ministries in England and abroad.

I also want to acknowledge Rev. Ricky Ramus of the Living Word International Ministries for being my friend and mentor in the early stages of my search for God. Thank you for being an inspiration to me and for speaking those prophetic words that gave birth to my ministry.

Contents

Chapter One 9
Singleness or Separation
Ruth's Story

Chapter Two 41
Rape
Dinah's Story

Chapter Three 75
Incest
Tamar's Story

Chapter Four 103
The 'Matey' Syndrome
Hannah's Story

Chapter Five 135
Just Want to Be Loved for Me...
Leah's Story

Chapter Six 169
A Mother's Love
Rizpah's Story

Chapter Seven **203**
Sensuality: Blessing or Curse?
Delilah's Story

Chapter Eight **249**
The Ultimate Plan 'B'
Eve's Story

Introduction

This book has been written for women everywhere, all around the world. By writing about godly Biblical women and how their struggles were not so different from ours, I hope to reveal the truth that the Bible is still as contemporary and as relevant a guide for life today as it was centuries ago.

Life in modern times can seem so difficult and so far removed from Biblical times. This is especially true for women today, as we are forced to take on a variety of roles. We are often only able to meet the hectic demands of life by multi tasking our way through a plethora of routine daily chores.

In the midst of all this, so many women spend their entire lives searching to find themselves and to find true love and acceptance. There is a built-in need to be loved for who we are and not based on what we can do or give. This inner longing transcends all the trappings of wealth, possessions and popularity, and it is not based on class or culture.

In chapter 9 of this book, we will look at the story of Leah, who seems to have everything a woman could ever need or want. She was in a secure extended family environment, which also meant she was financially secure as a woman of her time, with a husband and children. Yet all she longed for was to be loved by her husband for who she was. Throughout her story, we see her struggle to find the magic key to pleasing her husband and winning his love. Yet she had to watch painfully as his other wife, Rachel, was able to melt his heart with a simple smile.

The profile of the 21st century woman takes many forms; she may be portrayed as a driven, hard-core career woman who has sacrificed motherhood or relationships for the sake of her profession. She may even be a single mother raising a family on her own and struggling to provide as the main or sometimes the only breadwinner. Sometimes even when they are in a relationship, many women still find themselves having to shoulder a large share of the burden. They often have to double up their roles, and act as both homemaker and breadwinner for the family.

For many women, this often means leaving their full time paid job at the end of the day only to go home and work at their unpaid full time job, one that starts the minute they get home and begin to prepare the evening meal. This job does not end until they finally collapse into bed after making sure their family is settled for the night. For some this is not even the end of the workday, as it may be the only time left to give their partner the last shreds of their energy and attention. This may be done in a feeble attempt to keep the relationship whole or to obey their marital vows. No wonder so many women feel tired, helpless, anxious, stressed out, and depressed. There is an overwhelming feeling that there really must be more to life than this.

Traditional roles seem to have gone out the window long ago. Many women find it difficult to relate to what life must have been like in Old Testament times or even what Christianity may have been like in the first centuries after

Just Want to be Loved for Me...

Christ's death and resurrection. Many people also feel that the lives of the various women portrayed in different books of the Bible are not relevant or contemporary. They therefore assume those Biblical women's lives have very little bearing on how women experience life now. It is hard to imagine that women of times past would have had to struggle with the complex family relationships we face today.

Very little is known about some of the Biblical women we'll be discussing in this book. They have often been upstaged by their more famous male counterparts. Everyone seems to know the stories of Abraham, Isaac and Jacob or of King David, the famous shepherd boy who became king; likewise for his equally famous son King Solomon, who was renowned for his wisdom. Yet, the famous godly women of the Bible are not given the same accolades.

Irrespective of that oversight, their contributions remain important; furthermore, the fact that their stories are included in the Bible is not an accident. There are great lessons to be learnt from studying them. There is also the opportunity to see how their situations were crucial in enabling God's plan for humankind to be fulfilled.

Today, it does seem hard to imagine similarities between Biblical and modern women. For a start, single mothers are more commonplace, something that is now widely accepted. In Biblical times, single women were pitied and considered a burden on the extended family because they had very limited means to support themselves. Feeling the weight of this burden made it hard for them to feel accepted and loved. This also would have had a negative impact on their levels of confidence and self-esteem.

Modern children have become accustomed to having different homes and spending their time shifting between them after their parents have split up for any number of reasons. Cheating partners, heartbreak, financial and family strain are accepted as a normal part of life. We live in a world where emotional, physical and sexual abuse, paedophilia, pagan worship and the belief that man himself is God, is rife.

Even women from the more traditional cultural backgrounds find themselves struggling for acceptance. They struggle to engage with a world dominated by the seemingly sophisticated western ideals. They struggle with buying into its glamour and freedoms while staying true to the strict demands of their own more rigid culture. They battle daily with trying to drag their ancient ideals kicking and screaming into the twenty-first century. Yet at the same time, they want to remain true to who they are, and their culture is inherently a part of that.

This often leads to discontent, frustration and increased levels of anxiety as women struggle against the cultural barriers that separate them from the western phenomena of the independent woman who controls her own life and destiny. Even those who find such independence face a struggle to become accepted by either side – modernity and tradition – and often end up feeling torn and confused.

This image of the modern woman seems so far removed from the traditional image of the perfect or ideal woman as portrayed by Solomon in Proverbs chapter 31. This woman has the qualities that a large number of modern men use to measure whether or not a woman is worthy to receive his favours or even to qualify as his wife.

The Proverbs 31 Woman

For who can find a virtuous wife
For her worth is far above rubies
The heart of her husband safely trusts her

So he will have no lack of gain
She does him good and not evil
all the days of her life

Strength and honour are her clothing
She shall rejoice in time to come
She opens her mouth with wisdom
And on her tongue is the law of kindness

She watches over the ways of her household
And does not eat the bread of idleness
Her children rise up and call her blessed

Her husband also and he praises her
Many daughters have done well
but you excel them all

Charm is deceitful, beauty is passing
But a woman who fears the Lord
SHE shall be praised…

This woman seems to be so perfect. When she was written about, I believe it was with the intention of giving godly women something to aspire to. This ideal woman should be welcomed and admired by all. We all know that no one is perfect. Yet her qualities are still generally revered, even now in modern times, and are considered by many Christian men to be the standard by which all women should be measured. When most women are measured by this standard, however, they rarely make the grade.

However, it is important to note that the Proverbs 31 woman was definitely not meant as an ideal or a real person that women should fear or be intimidated by. Many modern women feel that they have to deny being what and who they are just so they can measure up to this ancient ideal. This also leaves them feeling unfulfilled as women of God. This is especially true when, despite their best efforts, they fail to walk in the Proverbs 31 woman's shoes consistently.

This clearly shows that the scripture has been misunderstood and misapplied. Modern women should take heart that the 'ideal' woman of God – a regular woman like you and me – is charged only with living her life productively and being a blessing to others. This is acceptable in the full variety of shapes or forms it may take.

When there is misunderstanding or lack of knowledge of the scriptures, all kinds of evils steps in to fill that void. Those who do not know the Bible well think that some of the things women suffer today are new and therefore there is no way the Bible could have something to say on the matter or help to lead them through their difficult times.

This is so far from the truth. As King Solomon also said in the book of Ecclesiastes, there is nothing new under the sun; the issues that we struggle with today are the same as the things women struggled with in Biblical times. The location may be different, and there may be slight differences having to do with cultural or even customary practices, but

Just Want to be Loved for Me...

there are many similarities between Biblical women and us. Just as in the days of old, women today still struggle to find a place where they can truly be themselves.

Be blessed as you read through this book and discover a God who created ***you*** out of love ... who wants ***you*** to fulfil the purpose he created ***you*** for ... and is a constant and unchanging force in ***your*** life – even now in this modern age !

Pray with me….

Father in heaven, I thank you for your love and for your many mercies in life and for the opportunity for me to be used to speak to your people.

Thank you, Lord, that you are the one constant thing in my life and that you never, ever change.

Today, Lord, I come into agreement with my sister or brother holding this book. Father, I ask that you will anoint each page and allow a special blessing to flow into their life as they read. Whatever their situation, I pray that you will intervene on their behalf and remove any barriers that may be holding them back. Open their hearts right now, Lord, so that they can hear from you and move forward in your love. Help them, Lord, to be able to understand you better and to clearly see how they can draw closer to you.

Show them, Lord, how they can live their lives according to the purpose that you created them for.

Father, I claim success and victory on their behalf right now in Jesus' name. I exalt your name in all things. Yours is the glory, the honour and the praise. Thank you, Lord, for hearing my prayer. In Jesus' name I pray, AMEN !

Chapter One

Singleness or Separation

Ruth's Story

Introduction – Being Single

Singleness may come in a variety of forms in modern times. It may be that women have not yet found their ideal partner and so remain single while they patiently wait for God's perfect will to be done in their lives. Some women are single because of divorce or separation from their long-term relationships. For others singleness is the result of a separation caused by death. More commonly, some of us face separation brought about because of moving from one place to another or from one country to another. This causes us to leave behind the places and people we are familiar with and have attachments to. Each of these states of separation has its own issues and difficulties.

We often feel there is a need to work through the issues surrounding separation and then just move on. The road to wholeness is a journey each person makes on his or her own. Even with all the best advice and support in the world, each one of us ultimately has to work things out on our own. It is often at this time that we feel alone, anxious or afraid in the knowledge that whatever we decide, and however we choose to move on, it will impact the rest of our lives. This is difficult at any age, but it becomes more onerous as we get older. Women fear that there is less room for error or learning curves. We actually just need to get it right this time. There is also the worry that we will continue to make the same mistakes again and again – that we may not have learned the lesson well enough because there is something lurking in our subconscious that makes us prone to falling into the same kind of situations we strive so hard to avoid.

There are issues to do with confidence and self-esteem that come from having to accept (albeit reluctantly) that the choices we made in the past were poor, and that maybe we are not as gifted in making the right decisions as we once thought we were.

What does the Bible have to say about this?

The Bible was set in a world where the family unit was so important, but women had very little to say about their own lives and future. This causes us to wonder how the Bible can relate to modern women who are struggling to cope with the single life.

Singleness during Biblical times was not exalted, and in fact was considered a socially inferior status. Single people were at the bottom of the pile. They faced economic hardships and social prejudice. Even now, we live with the image of the struggling single parent who is blamed for every social ill that faces society today. They are often also living in poverty and have socially excluded families. Often we see wonderful examples of children who have excelled despite coming from a single parent home. Singleness has now become so commonplace that it longer carries the huge stigma it used to.

Sometimes when we read of famous singles in the Bible, such as the apostle Paul, who states that he is glad he is single, we get the impression that they were self-assured and confident – not the quivering wrecks struggling for survival like the ordinary folk of today who feel as though they are a million times removed from such greatness.

When studying famous singles in the Bible, the obvious place to start seems to be at the story of Abraham, who was the founding father of the chosen nation. He was called by

Just Want to be Loved for Me...

God to leave his family and homeland to travel to a place that God would show him. In order for God to work in his life and to bless him, he had to be prepared to move away from all that was familiar to him. By taking him away from the people and the environment he had come from, God now had a blank sheet to work with, and the people in Abraham's past would not be able to affect God's plan for his life. There are untold nuggets of truth contained in Abraham's story and the eventful journey he had with his wife Sarai (who was later renamed Sarah). However, as this book is essentially about women, I will turn to look at another story that also shows the powerful working of an omnipotent God. You may wish to read Genesis chapter 12 in your spare time to learn about the story of Abraham and Sarah.

If we look at the story of Ruth, we see how God intervenes in a situation that seems so hopeless at the beginning and which could have had a disastrous outcome. We see how God orchestrates the events to allow Ruth to fulfil her destiny to become one of the great grandmothers in the line of Judah from which the Messiah would eventually come.

We know that we are all made to fulfil a purpose on earth. We are told this in Psalm chapter 139. This is one of my favourite psalms:

I praise you because I am fearfully and wonderfully made; your works are wonderful, I know that full well. My frame was not hidden from you when I was made in the secret place. When I was woven together in the depths of the earth, your eyes saw my unformed body. All the days ordained for me were written in your book before one of them came to be (Psalm 139:14-16 NIV).

This is so awesome because it tells us that God made each one of us individually and planned each day of our lives before he even made the days or the world. This means that he made us first.

This is a bit like making a cake. You would never just think, *I will make a cake right now* and then just make it. There will always be an element of planning. Will it be a fruitcake or a sponge, with icing or not, with jam or cream? To some extent, the purpose or occasion for making the cake will likely determine what kind it will be. For example, if the cake is for a wedding, it traditionally will be a fruitcake. However, you may decide you want this occasion to be different, and so you make a sponge without icing.

Once you decide what kind of cake it will be, and what occasion you will make it for, whether it is for a dessert, birthday or wedding, you will then decide what ingredients you will need. You will make sure that you have them in your cupboard or else you will have to buy them before you start. This is called the planning process. Next comes the operational stage, and this is when you will actually make the cake. Again, there are tricks to the trade here too. For example, you may beat the eggs and the sugar together for longer if you are making a sponge to make sure that there is enough air beaten into it. However, you would not need to concentrate on this so much if you were making a fruitcake. The last stage is the presentation of your baking skills and the enjoyment of eating the cake. You will only know if you have been successful if the taste, texture, and appearance of the cake matches up to what you planned for in the beginning, and only then will you know whether you can use it for the purpose you intended.

Just Want to be Loved for Me...

If we go through such an involved process to make a simple cake, why should it be so hard to understand that God did this when he created each one of us? We all know how complex the human body is, and we are still mystified by how the mind and spiritual side of us works within our body. It blows my mind just thinking about this! It seems incredible that God knows every element of each day of my life and that he planned it that way before I was born. Psalm 139:14 begins with the acknowledgement that God knows me and every part of me. It asks the question of where one can go to escape from God, because wherever you go, he will still be there. This acknowledges the omnipotence of God and the fact that he is all seeing and all knowing.

In the corner of your mind, I hear you asking, *If this is really true, and God knew ahead of time that I would experience all the awful things I have been through, then why did he allow them to happen in the first place?*

Well, there are two things to understand here. First of all, sometimes it is the negative things we have been through that make us the person we are right now. Suppose God were to say to you, *My child, I have chosen you to be a woman of leadership, understanding and passion. You will bless many people and will offer great support to them; your life will be an example and a light to others.* Wouldn't we all be really happy to be chosen for a blessing like this?

What would your response be if he then told you that as a preparation for this important work, you must first endure financial hardship to the point where you lose the roof over your head and become destitute...

...That your heart must be broken many times by men you have loved with all your heart...

..… and you must suffer the loss of friendships as people you love or care about let you down over and over again.

Would you still be jumping up and down saying, 'Me, me Lord, pick me!'

I know for a fact that I would never have chosen to go through some of the very painful things I've endured in my life. No one volunteers for pain or misery, unless of course you are Jesus. Therefore, it is sometimes better for us if we do not know what our future holds.

The second point to consider is that even though we may be totally surprised at what is going to happen today, whether it is good or bad, it is awesome to realise that God already knows. He planned it, and even the fact that you are reading this book right now was already planned. Whatever you learn from it and how it will affect your life has already been planned by God. This goes right back to the heart of relationships. If God made you and knows what is going to happen, and if he is the only one who ultimately can change or affect things in your life, then it makes perfect sense not to try to run your own life. Instead, you should be developing a close relationship with God.

Stop worrying about your life or your future, and whether things make sense or not, and stop trying to engineer your future alone. Let go and let God take over. It is so liberating to rest in the knowledge that whatever is taking place in your life, God is with you and already knows this was going to happen. He alone can take you to the next level so that

Just Want to be Loved for Me...

you can move on. Stop fighting against the tide. Let the flow of his healing love, grace and protection sail you through the cares of life.

Ruth's story

Her name means 'beautiful', and she represents all that is good and positive. Ruth's story is so awesome, that there **had** to be a divine plan in place. There is no other explanation. Yet there is no way that Ruth's destiny could have been foreseen by any human being. She was not even born into the right family. She was instead born as a Moabite, and as such was a direct descendant of children born from an incestuous liaison. This was because God delivered his judgement on the cities of Sodom and Gomorrah. After they were destroyed, Lot escaped with his family. Lot's two daughters ended up being alone with him, stranded away from any form of civilisation. The daughters panicked that they would never be able to have children and carry on the family line. They feared that they would live long, lonely and unfulfilled lives. Only death would be a welcome release from this unpalatable situation. They got together and planned a way to make sure that this would never happen. Lot's daughters decided to get him drunk in order to have sex with him, and hopefully get pregnant so that they could carry on the family line. The plan was a successful one, and new nations were created from this liaison. You can learn more about this story in the book of Genesis chapter 19.

This background made Ruth an unlikely candidate for marriage into the Messiah's bloodline. This is exactly what happened, however: Ruth married Naomi's son. This in itself was out of the ordinary, as it was specifically forbidden for God's chosen people to marry foreign wives. The Moabites worshipped other gods and did not know or recognise the God of the Israelites. They were afraid that by marrying these women, the hearts of men would be drawn toward these other gods and their own God would be forgotten. Naomi's son chose to disobey this rule and married Ruth.

At the start of the story, we find that Ruth is widowed, without any children of her own. She is left with her husband's mother Naomi and her sister in law, Orpah, both of whom were also widowed. Women were looked after by their fathers before marriage and by their husbands afterward. By law, the two girls were Naomi's responsibility now that her sons had died. She was widowed herself, with no resources of her own, and thus she could not provide for them. They would now be forced to live on handouts if there were no other male relatives to care for them. This would cause great physical and emotional hardship for the women.

To spare them from this fate, Naomi told Orpah and Ruth to go back to their families and throw themselves on their mercy. She had reached the end of her line and did not know what else to do. Her options were very limited at this stage of her life. Once her daughters-in-law had returned to their families, she planned to go back to her homeland to die alone. She would be back on familiar ground, but she would be returning as a failure with nothing to show for her life. Her intentions were selfless and were based on her need to protect Orpah and Ruth and to ensure that they would be looked after. She was more concerned about them than she was about herself, partly because she felt that her life was over anyway.

Just Want to be Loved for Me...

Orpah is obedient and decides to go back to her people. Interestingly enough, the name Orpah means 'hair or hide'. It seems to be a very strange name to give someone, especially a daughter. In their culture names were very important and always had meaning. I am reminded that hair needs certain conditions for it to flourish. For example, dry hair needs moisture or it will break, and greasy hair renders hair dull and lifeless. Just like the meaning of her name, Orpah needed the conditions to be right to stay with Ruth and her mother-in-law.

She chose to return to a life of certainty with her family rather than follow Naomi to a strange land and culture. Although she had loved her husband, she had never been fully committed to his ways and his strange invisible God. His family were strangers to her land, but that partly explained why she was drawn to him. It was refreshing to meet someone who was different even if his family ways seemed a little unusual to her. Chilion was technically not a stranger anyway, since he was born in her homeland and understood her people's ways. It always gave her a little edge over the other girls that her husband was different and had a mysterious background and foreign religion. His ways didn't really have much of an impact on her anyway. She was still able to worship with her family and friends as before. She had the best of both worlds.

Sometimes we see people missing out on a blessing or opportunities because they are afraid to be in situations that make them feel unsure. This is because like Orpah, they will choose the safer and less risky options. Again, this is determined by the relationship you have with God and how much you truly believe that he knows what is best for you.

More importantly, when you are willing to take risks based on the certainty that you are in God's will, and you are willing to step out in faith to embrace something you are not sure about, you will most likely discover that it is only in this type of situation that He is able to introduce the changes in you that will bring forth the blessing you have been praying for.

The story is so different for Ruth. Despite her pagan upbringing, she found herself wholeheartedly cleaving to her husband and honouring her marital vows. This means that she became one with him, embracing all that he was. She got to know all about his cultural and religious beliefs. Ruth was able to enjoy a personal, spiritual relationship with his God that she had never experienced before with her pagan gods. This made her a little estranged from her family. They were unable to understand how she had switched her loyalties to a God that no one could see. They still had a relationship with her but they prayed that she would soon snap out of this 'phase' she was going through. They thought their prayers and sacrifices to their gods had been answered when Ruth's husband Mahlon died and her future came into question. They felt sure that things would change and that she would now return to her former life and take up her 'rightful place' with her people.

Ruth is a very determined young lady and is clear about what she wants. She refuses to leave and ends up staying with Naomi. She is filled with love and compassion for the plight of her mother in law, and therefore, she cannot imagine walking away from her in this situation. Naomi has become more than 'just' Ruth's mother in law; she is her friend and mentor as well. Ruth's words have become famous because they represent the ultimate display of commitment,

Just Want to be Loved for Me...

loyalty and love that one person can have for another. I have attended many weddings where the bride and groom have used these words to declare the strength of their love and their commitment to sharing a long life together.

Ruth says to Naomi:

Entreat me not to leave you, or to turn back from following after you, for wherever you go, I will go, and wherever you lodge, I will lodge. Your people shall be my people and your God my God. Where you die, I will die and there will I be buried. The Lord do so to me and more also… if anything but death parts you and me (Ruth 1:16-17).

It is easy to see how a groom's heart would melt with love and pride to hear his new bride vow these tender words to him. These are the very ingredients that make a good start to any couple's married life together. Wedding guests are also deeply touched to be so privileged to witness such fresh, newfound love and devotion being conveyed through words such as these.

In Ruth's case, how can Naomi refuse such heartfelt words? That Ruth could speak so sincerely from her heart shows how much Ruth has changed, having been introduced to God through her in-laws. She is prepared to leave behind all that she knows and is familiar with to follow Naomi. She has fully embraced Naomi's God, her people and her customs.

Back in the family homeland

Naomi arrives home with mixed emotions. She is happy to be back in familiar surroundings but sad because of the circumstances that have brought her home. As she wanders through her village, she notices how different everything looks, and she marvels at all the changes that have been made in her absence. She also notices many strange faces that she has never seen. Despite its basic familiarity, in many ways it feels like a foreign land to her. She is suddenly filled with fear, and the newness of everything makes her feel uncomfortable. She seriously thinks of turning back. However, the sensible side of her knows that she has very few options, and turning back is definitely not one of them.

As Naomi and Ruth walk down the main road through the village, they see people turning their heads to look at them as they pass by. They are strangers, and people are wondering who they are and what business they have there. They whisper amongst themselves and try to guess who these women are, but more than that, the townspeople wonder who they have come to see. The two women look so tired and weary, and it is obvious that they have come a long way.

A group of older women sitting under the shade of a nearby tree stare intently at Naomi as she walks past them; they can't help wondering who she is. Suddenly a couple of them pause, their foreheads creased as they struggle to remember something. Within seconds their faces light up with a flicker of recognition as they realise this is their old friend Naomi. Still feeling uncertain, they look to each other eagerly for confirmation, whispering and nodding with broadening smiles on their faces.

It had all been so long ago. If she was who they thought she was, then they were shocked to see how dishevelled and worn down she looked. They studied her face and

Just Want to be Loved for Me...

remembered Naomi as a beautiful young woman. She had been so alive and vibrant. She had left them and moved away with her husband Elimelech during the famine many years ago. Those were hard times for everyone, and there seemed to be no sign of relief for their nation. Naomi and her husband had been so sure that they would find their fortunes if they moved away. They felt that they had no future if they stayed. In any event, they were a stunning couple and were so much in love. They had refused to heed any warnings about any possible danger they may face if they moved away. As far as they were concerned, they had each other, and that was all that mattered to them. It would be better to die trying than to remain in a familiar land and die a slow and painful death from starvation. They had been the envy of many as they refused to allow fear to dictate the course of their life together.

By now, the women were almost sure it was Naomi, and as they scrambled up and clustered around her, they had a million and one questions to ask her. They had always wondered if she had really fared better than they had done by staying. After Naomi and her husband had left, many others had followed suit, but fear had kept a lot of them right there on familiar ground. They had chosen to suffer in silence, unable to move forward or to accept change. Fear of the unknown had seriously gripped them. In the long hard years that followed, they had gone from regretting not having left, to justifying themselves for sticking it out through the hard times.

As the women greet Naomi, they eagerly examine every inch of her worn and weathered face. She looks so old and weary now, and the lines etched on her face betray the fact that she is not doing well and that life has not been very kind to her. Her clothes are faded and worn. Her brow is furrowed by worry lines. Her eyes are large and sunken into sad pools of misery and despair. Yet there is no mistaking that this is Naomi. Beneath it all, they still see the remnants of the ravishing beauty that left their shores all those years ago. They notice that she is accompanied by a young lady who they assume is her daughter, a beautiful girl with large attractive eyes that are also filled with sadness. She too seems very weary from her travels.

"Is that really you, Naomi?" they ask. Naomi manages a forced smile, relieved at last to see some familiar faces. These women were girls she had grown up with and laughed with, and together they had dreamed of a future filled with romance, prosperity and children. She greets them and tells them with much sadness in her voice that she has changed her name from Naomi, which means 'pleasant', to Mara, which means 'bitter'. This describes how she sees herself now after the cruel blows that life seems to have dealt her.

She is at an all–time low point now and has gone way past the stage where she feels the need to impress anyone anymore. She clearly remembers leaving Bethlehem with her husband Elimelech all those years ago because of the famine that had gripped the land. That had been when the judges were the ruling body and the people were being warned again and again to keep the laws of God faithfully. God had visited his judgement upon them because of their disobedience to him. Things had become so hard for everyone, and in desperation, people left in droves in search of a better life.

Elimelech and Naomi had moved to the land of Moab in search of a better life, fleeing hardship and hoping to find

Just Want to be Loved for Me...

a better way to survive. Elimelech loved his new wife with all his heart. He had been so protective of her and wanted her to have the best that life could offer. As a young couple, they had left full of hope and anticipation that wherever they ended up they would be able to raise their family under better circumstances. Naomi adored her husband as much as he loved her, and she would have gladly gone to the ends of the earth with him if he had asked her to.

I find it interesting that they chose to go to the land of Moab, which was a place where the people did not know God. By choosing this location, their children and thus the next generation inevitably would grow up among pagan worshippers. This does not seem to be the right actions for a man such as Elimelech, whose name means 'God is King'. Keep in mind that they were leaving home because of the judgement of God on their people. It seems an odd choice that they would seek solace in a pagan land. True, things would be better for them physically and materially in this land. However, it actually got worse for them in terms of their spirituality. Their two precious sons grew up among Moabites and of course chose to marry Moabite women, and this directly contravened the laws of God.

It was hard for Naomi to tell whether it was just bad luck or God's judgement that had fallen upon her. She became widowed when Elimelech died, but at least the boys were there to look after her, and they took their role very seriously in doing so. However, within a relatively short time, they too died, and for the first time in her life, Naomi was left to fend for herself. In addition, as the head of the family, she now had to shoulder the responsibility for her two daughters in law. Naomi had very little to celebrate or to even be happy about with this burden on her. It was very much a man's world at that time, and women without male relatives were a liability to the community.

So here she is, back in her homeland with nothing to call her own. She is driven by her need to survive against all the odds. Gone are her dreams of returning home to retire after living a successful life in another place. She is hurt, broken and disappointed. Nothing has gone the way she planned when she was young and hopeful, full of excitement at the possibilities stretching before her. Her dreams are shattered, and now she faces a very uncertain future.

This reminds me of the separation faced by many families that have left their homelands in search of a better life in a foreign country. Often they are motivated to leave the familiar for the unknown because of their discontentment with the life they currently have, and they know there *must* be something better on the horizon. Often times they are driven by harsh social, economic and financial conditions that severely restrict and limit the progress they can make in their home country. They desperately want something more for themselves and their children and are willing to pay the price for it. So, they leave a life they know very well to go to a strange place where the grass seems to be oh so much greener than it is in the land they're leaving behind, all this despite the fact that they will most likely not be welcomed by the local people in their newly adopted country. Their initial hope and excitement is often received with hostility and mistrust from the local people. Yet the promise of being able to achieve their dream enables them to face any condition head on. This is with their absolute conviction that the move will only be a temporary solution to a pressing problem they are facing, and soon they will return to their homeland.

Just Want to be Loved for Me...

My family's story in the 1960s

My family came to Britain in the sixties leaving behind their life in Jamaica. They came in search of a better life and access to opportunities they could only dream about back home. They had a firm plan in mind. They would stay for five years, living on the absolute minimum while they scrimped and saved. At the end of the period, they planned to go back home and then set themselves up in business and secure a comfortable life for themselves and their children. At the end of five years, my parents actually achieved this goal and went back to Jamaica to start their business.

For many families, the dream of going back never materialised as real life took over, responsibilities grew and hardships set in. Things had not worked out the way they hoped. Out of pride, they would never face going home with nothing. They would never accept that they had failed. They would never accept or admit to themselves or to the families back home that things had not worked out. The letters they wrote home would be full of joy, hope and success stories of the wonderful life they had managed to acquire. Meanwhile, they were struggling and scraping along, hanging on by a thread and longing for home.

Before going home on holiday, they would work and save for months to be sure that the impression they gave when they got home was one of success; they wanted everyone to be certain of how well they were doing. The extended family would never know the truth. The heartache of having failed, and the constant struggles they endured to make ends meet, was a well-kept secret. How much they missed their homeland, and how trapped they felt in a foreign land that had become their reluctant home, was never revealed to their families.

Even today, we see families torn apart, uprooted and forced to flee borders because of political upheaval, war and famine. They arrive as refugees, often with very little more than the clothes on their backs. They are traumatised and anguished, often having been tortured and imprisoned, and seeking a safe haven in a strange new land because they have in essence lost their families anyway. For them the pain of separation is one that can never be resolved, as they are in a position where they are unable to return home, ever, for fear of being killed. They too are trapped in a hostile place that must become their reluctant home.

It is easy to understand what Naomi was feeling as she returned to her homeland. Can you identify with Naomi's plight?

Boaz gives favour

It doesn't take Naomi very long to find her way around the area and to find somewhere to stay. She and Ruth then have to find a way to survive. Because they have no male relatives to take care of them, this could prove to be very difficult. Ruth decides to take things into her own hands. It is harvest time and people are very busy reaping the barley fields. She goes to a nearby field and joins in with some of the other people who are working there collecting the 'gleanings' or the bits that are left at the edges of the fields after the reapers have finished their work. (It was a common practice for the owner to instruct his workers to reap only to a certain part in the field. This gave the opportunity for

Just Want to be Loved for Me...

the crops at the edge of the field to be collected and used by the poorer people in the area.)

Boaz, the wealthy owner of the field, becomes very much aware of the beautiful, young stranger who consistently gleans from his field every day. He notices that Ruth is a strong girl who is not afraid of hard work. He wonders who she is and begins to make enquiries. In a place like Bethlehem, it didn't take very long for him to get the full story. Everyone seemed to know who she was. Her beauty and pleasing manner had impressed many people, and this was only added to when they realised that she was single and had chosen to stay with Naomi.

When Boaz realises who she is and therefore understands the problems that Ruth and Naomi must be facing, his heart is softened and he grants favour to Ruth by telling his workers to leave extra gleanings so that she can collect them. He also finds opportunities to talk to her and really starts to take an interest in this lovely young woman. By now, he is mesmerised by her beauty and is especially attracted to her large brown eyes that seem to hold his gaze. She also has a warm and cheeky smile that lights up her whole face, and he finds himself unable to tear himself away from her whenever they have a chance meeting. He often makes silly excuses to talk to her, just to be near her and to have her undivided attention, even if just for a few minutes.

He extends his favour by telling her to stay with the young women of his field and not to go to the other field to glean. This provides her the opportunity to have access to food and drink. Boaz takes his concern for Ruth a step further: he offers her his protection from anyone who would seek to harm her.

This was important for Ruth. As a young single woman, she could have easily fallen prey to the local young men who often harassed and teased the younger women. It would also make suitors think twice before approaching her. They would now be more likely to have serious intentions and not just be hoping to have a bit of fun with a sexy young stranger.

Ruth is understandably humbled by his favour, especially since she is a foreigner and in a strange land where everything is so different. As a man of God, Boaz recognises her efforts in taking care of her mother in law, and he understands what she has been through in losing her husband and her home.

The art of seduction

What happens next is crucial in bringing this story to a happy ending. I am sure that women all over the world can identify with it. When Naomi finds out what Boaz has done for Ruth, she begins to educate Ruth to use her womanly skills to seduce him. Again, Naomi is driven by a selfless need to make sure that Ruth's future will be secured.

Somehow, as Christians and 'decent' women, we often become asexual in our attitude and behaviour. We seem to suppress our ability to be sexy, captivating and alluring. We come across as pure, holy, strong and capable. There is nothing wrong with these qualities, but as females, there is definitely another side to us. It would be hard for me to imagine many of the Christian women I grew up with being sexy, captivating and alluring. Yet these are key elements that God himself placed within every woman, and we long

Just Want to be Loved for Me...

to be pursued, adored and desired by men. These are natural aspects of our physical and mental makeup, and as such, should not be taken lightly. The only question is whether you will use your God-given femininity to achieve good or to achieve selfish or negative ends. 'Decent' young girls are groomed to not delight in or express their sexual nature. For Christian women in general, our identity as sexual beings is sometimes portrayed as something we should be ashamed of. After all, look where it got Eve. Equipped with a brand new womanly body, the very embodiment of sensuality and sexuality, she used her feminine wiles to tempt her poor mindless husband. This event led to the ultimate fall of man.

Naomi tells Ruth that Boaz is actually a male relative of Ruth's husband Mahlon. She explains that under the rights of kinship laws, he is obliged to marry her. He was also compelled by law to raise children in the name Ruth's dead husband so that his lineage would not die. However, this law was only relevant if there was not a closer male relative who was willing or able to marry her. These kinship laws were a serious matter, and males were obliged to obey them to preserve the family. Under the Jewish law, if a kinsman refused to honour these laws, a widow had the right to bring this reluctant relative to the elders of the area. Pressure would be brought to bear on him to compel him to obey. However, if he still refused to marry the widow, he would be publicly shamed, which would bring great dishonour on his own family. You can read about this more fully in the book of Deuteronomy, specifically in chapter 25 from verse 7 onwards.

In this situation, we see that God is about to bring redemption from the difficult circumstances Ruth and

Naomi have endured, and we can also see how God's blessings for his people flow through the generations.

Naomi uses her wisdom to set in motion a plan that will secure Ruth's future and ultimately her own. She sets Ruth on a mission of seduction. She already has a good relationship with Ruth. They had often shared secrets, and Naomi had often provided Ruth with advice and support. This time was no different, and if the plan worked well, things could really be turned around for them.

Naomi tells Ruth to get washed, perfumed and dressed in her best clothes. Once Ruth is ready, she is to go to the field where Boaz will be working that night. She is not to make him aware of her presence. It was customary after working so late into the night for the workers to eat together, and they usually consumed lots of drink. Most of the time they were so exhausted and intoxicated that they would just find a spot in the field where they could bed down and sleep for the night. This meant that they would also be on site to fend off any robbers who might happen along. In any case, the workers were rarely able to make it home to a comfortable bed after their long hours of labouring in the fields.

Being familiar with this customary practice, Naomi instructs Ruth that when she sees that Boaz has finished eating and drinking, she is to pay careful attention to where he lies down to rest. Once she is sure that he has settled down for the night, she is to uncover his feet, lie down next to them and wait. Once he becomes aware of her, she should follow his instructions. Under Jewish custom, lying at a man's feet signified a woman's willingness to surrender completely to his will. If he agreed to be her covering in life, he would then throw the covers over her in a symbolic gesture that she was under his protection.

The perfect plan

Ruth understands exactly what she must do, and she realises the importance of the task ahead. This is 'make or break time' and she is determined to succeed. I can see Ruth now, dressed for success, her young body perfumed and clad in her best clothes, her hair and makeup carefully done without flaw. If she had been going to a ball, I am sure she definitely would have been in the Cinderella category. She follows Naomi's instructions exactly and lies down at Boaz's feet. You can imagine the scene at midnight when Boaz turns over in his sleep and is startled to discover a live, warm and sexy woman at his feet. He hears the rustle of her best clothes, smells the allure of her feminine scent and feels the softness of her body against his feet.

He is already in a mellow mood brought on by the copious amount of wine he has just consumed and is even more excited when he realises that it is Ruth at his feet. Remember, he is already attracted to her, and he has given her much favour.

We do not know if he ever intended to make a move on Ruth; maybe he was planning to but was simply not ready yet. Ruth's actions, though, are designed to speed up the process and to offer a little subtle encouragement. In this cosy, physical position, she begins a conversation with him. She makes full use of the fact that he has a full stomach, is merry from the wine and now has a beautiful, sexy woman at his feet ready to do his bidding. What more could a man want?

Ruth, however, has a clear outcome in mind and is ready to pursue it. She strikes up a conversation with him, and it is during the course of this dialogue that she brings up the issue of kinship rights and asks him to take her under his wing as a close relative under those rights. She holds her breath, her heart beats faster and faster, and her mouth feels dry and parched as she anxiously awaits his reply. This is the moment of truth; this will tell her whether her efforts have all been in vain.

She need not have worried, though, because she was pretty much onto a winner at the start. She already has so many things going for her. She is seeking a way to move her life on and to survive through this difficult situation. She is not aware of the great plan God has for her as she awaits Boaz's decision to accept her, but she senses that she is on the brink of walking into the destiny for which she was created.

Boaz has a positive response to her request. He begins to open his heart to her and share with her the feelings he has for her. He now confirms that he has been watching her all along and has taken time out to find out as much as he can about her in the hope that one day she would be his wife. Apart from her being the beautiful foreign visitor who has recently come to his land, Boaz also tells her that he has been attracted by the fact that she is highly blessed; he knows that she is a virtuous woman. Her behaviour has been of the highest order. He notices that she did not try to go after the other rich, young men to secure her future. He is flattered that she would look to him, an older man, for covering and protection, and that she would allow him to lavish his love and attention on her.

Just Want to be Loved for Me...

He is impressed that as a foreigner she has actually chosen to be obedient to the rules of kinship. In the short space of time that Ruth has been around, he has heard other people saying good things about her. He knows of her decision to forsake her own homeland and to follow Naomi. He also knows that she has accepted his God and has vowed to live as one of his own people would.

This situation allows Boaz and Ruth to develop a level of closeness and intimacy that sets the scene for what happens next. The Bible does not say explicitly whether there was a sexual encounter between them or not. Considering all that I have come to know about Ruth and the prevailing culture of that time, I believe that there was not a sexual encounter between them. Ruth is a woman on a mission, and giving herself to him completely would have caused her to lose the competitive edge. There would have been no incentive for him to keep his word if he had already managed to have her intimately. Remember also that he thinks she is a woman of virtue; therefore, if she had given herself to him without thought, it probably would have made him reconsider his opinion.

I believe that she used her feminine wiles to whet his appetite enough for him to be very interested in being intimate with her, but she left him willing to do whatever it would take to win her as the final prize. In addition, as his name suggests, he is indeed 'reliable, trustworthy and strong'. He will not abuse his position, especially when he knows that there is a potential problem to deal with first.

Kinship laws

This problem occurs because there is a relative other than Boaz who is closer to Ruth's dead husband, Mahlon. Boaz is only able to marry her if the other relative chooses not to. He promises to sort it out the next day and assures her that if the other relative does not want to marry her, then he will happily accept her as his wife.

Ruth settles down and stays with him for the rest of the night, but discreetly gets up early in the morning before everyone else. Doing so protects her reputation and keeps the private matters between them a secret from the others. Boaz provides for her again by filling her shawl with barley before she leaves to return home to Naomi. I imagine her leaving him in the silence of the new day and tiptoeing home as quietly as she could, probably hugging the barley-filled shawl to her body. Her steps are as light as her heart, her face bathed with a secret smile as she remembers the night before. With every step, she gives praise to God, hurrying her steps a little in her impatience to reach home so she can tell Naomi all that has happened.

Naomi has spent the night restlessly praying that everything would go according to plan. As the hours passed by with no sign of Ruth's early return, her hopes rise. She dozed fitfully throughout the night and now greets the dawn with her heart full of anticipation. She longs for the good news that can bring the changes they need so badly. She is hopeful because Ruth did not return early. This means that Boaz has not rejected Ruth outright. As the old saying goes, no news is good news.

Just Want to be Loved for Me...

The next day, true to his word, Boaz approaches the other male relative in front of the elders. He tells them about Naomi and the land that was owned by her husband Elimelech. Boaz asks the relative to buy the land belonging to Elimelech to redeem it on behalf of the family, or else he (Boaz) will. In the first instance, the relative readily agrees to buy the land, as this will enhance his own wealth. However, he swiftly changes his mind when he realises that he will also have to marry Ruth to redeem her dead husband Mahlon's lineage. He knows that this will mean that he will have to raise children with Ruth in Mahlon's name and is afraid that doing so will ruin his own inheritance. He decides this is too high a price to pay for the land he would receive as a part of this deal. He tells Boaz that he (Boaz) should buy the land and marry Ruth instead. This is all that Boaz needs to hear. He is now able to follow his heart freely and marry Ruth without dishonour. In line with the custom of the day, the relative takes off his sandal and gives it to Boaz as a cultural sign of their agreement in front of the elders as witnesses.

The elders respond by giving their blessing to Boaz and his union with Ruth. This is also witnessed by people who are standing in the gates of the building where the elders are gathered. It is a joyous occasion and many blessings are pronounced upon Ruth, who is now welcomed into the family. This means that she is no longer a foreigner in a strange land and is now a fully-fledged member of the family of God.

So after all the suffering that Naomi and Ruth had endured (and it is possible that Boaz had spent many lonely years of waiting before meeting Ruth, his true soul mate), we have a happy ending when Boaz marries Ruth. This is a fulfilment of God's plan for her life. She is finally able to walk into her destiny, and her situation has been fully turned around. Together they have a son called Obed. He would eventually have a son named Jesse, who would have a son named David. It is directly from King David's line that Jesus Christ, the Messiah, was to be born much later.

Ruth's loyalty to Naomi and her obedience to the Lord placed her in the lineage of Jesus Christ!

What about Naomi?

She also attains a life of security for herself, as she will live with Ruth and Boaz. Her fortunes have turned around and she will no longer be forced to live on charity or to die alone and miserable. The other women tell her that she is blessed by the God who never left her. She can now freely return to her original name of Naomi because her life is truly pleasant and filled with blessings.

This story is still relevant today

No matter what kind of family or circumstances you are born into, God can still lead you towards your destiny. You have been made in God's likeness, for a purpose, even if you do not yet know what that purpose is. Today, you need to surrender your life and your will to God. You need to give him permission to take over and take control. You must be ready to allow him to do whatever he needs to do in order to bring you to where you should be, even if that means you are to remain single or alone. In fact, the Apostle Paul spoke very highly about those who are single. He was one of the greatest leaders of the early Christian church, and he made a conscious choice to remain single so that he would have no distractions from serving God and doing God's work.

Just Want to be Loved for Me...

With all the difficulties and issues that women face in modern times, I found it so liberating when I realised that I really did not need to worry incessantly. I remember being told so often, "Why worry when you can pray?" Unfortunately, for many years I was not in a position to understand or even to accept that truth, which meant that although the words were encouraging, they were actually quite empty to me at the time. As an adult, I have felt under pressure at times to make things happen and to orchestrate my own life towards attaining set goals that surely would make me a 'success'. Whenever the pressure has been too much, I have often wished that I could go back home to my parents and just be a child again without responsibilities.

Today, there is so much comfort in knowing that I am moving toward my destiny and that God is with me to guide me, support me and strengthen me. He is in charge of my life and my destiny. This takes away the constant strife and worry I used to face. I know now that when I am weak, **he** will be my strength. When I am troubled, **he** will be my peace. When I am sick, **he** will be my healer, and when I am hurt or confused, **he** will comfort me.

More importantly, I know that when I feel lost and don't know which way to turn to face the lesser of the evils, I know that I can just be still and know that **he** is God and that I need to allow him to work in my life on my behalf. What more could I want than this reassurance. As I said earlier, this knowledge has liberated me from the self-imposed chains that once held me down. Now, at last, I truly am ***free***!

Chapter Two

Rape

Dinah's Story

Introduction

In this chapter, we will look at the incidence of rape and date rape, both of which still threaten and plague women in modern times. It is hard for anyone to understand the traumas associated with being raped unless they have actually experienced it. The shame and humiliation suffered as a result are second to none: the haunting memories that rewind and play over and over again in the recesses of your mind; the smell and sounds associated with the attacker; seeing men whose physical appearance is similar to the attacker – all make recovery a slow and painful process.

These crimes are primarily committed against women to subdue, humiliate and violate them in every possible sense, especially considering that molestation and rape are brutal acts that literally invade the secret parts of a girl or woman's body. These private parts were meant to be mutually enjoyed by a woman and her chosen marriage partner, not by a stranger who has inflicted an act of rage and hatred to exert his power and authority over her. Rape occurs when a woman is forced to endure sexual intercourse with a man against her will. Oftentimes this is accompanied by violence, force or other forms of sexual abuse. On most occasions, the attacker is unknown to the victim

I am reminded that when God created Eve, he did so while Adam was asleep. This meant that Adam was not privy to the intricate details of her physical, emotional and spiritual make up. God created her with secrets that were meant to be discovered by her chosen partner within the realms of their stable and loving relationship. These were intimate secrets that, when shared, created an unbreakable bond between them. This bond is still there between husbands and wives to this day, and sometimes these 'soul ties' may last long after the relationship has ended.

These secrets include the secret entrances that allow the man and the woman to become joined as one. It also allows partners to share the intimate details of their sexual preferences: for example, how, when and where they like to be touched, kissed or stroked, or even which positions they prefer to make love in. Partners are able to bond with each other in their most vulnerable and natural state, which they have reserved for each other and not shared with the outside world. This is why the violation and invasion caused by unlawful acts of violence or rape are so hard to overcome mentally and emotionally.

Date rape occurs when a woman consents to being in the same place as her attacker. This may be in the form of a legitimate date, a visit, or their agreed upon attendance at a social function. This situation is made unlawful when a man uses this opportunity to force the woman to have sexual intercourse with him. A woman may agree to be on a date or to have male company. This does not automatically mean that she consents to having sex as a by-product of enjoying his company.

Our newspapers and headlines are filled with stories warning women of the dangers they face when drugs are slipped into their drinks by men (or when they're simply pressured to swallow some pills) to make date rape easier. These drugs include tablets or liquids that when consumed through drink have the effect of causing the woman to relax to the point where she may lose her self-control and submit to the will of her attacker. In worse case scenarios, she may lose consciousness and wake up the next day with no memory of what happened to her the night before. The telltale signs of leftover bodily fluids, bruises or pain are the only clues to the invasion her body has experienced.

We know that the trauma of being raped has the power to negatively consume and destroy lives, and it is one of the most heinous crimes inflicted upon women. It is also not a new crime; stories of rape have been recorded throughout human history.

It is not a new phenomenon. It is more likely the case that because of new technology we are able to hear about it more readily as it gets reported on by the media.

I have also heard people talk about the growing incidence of male rape as a relatively new phenomena. Again, this is not the case. Our present law makes it an offence to commit sodomy, and this word is taken directly from the reference in the Old Testament to the immoral acts being committed in the cities of Sodom and Gomorrah. The events are clearly recorded in the book of Genesis in the Bible. Both cities were destroyed in a judgement from God. This is because of the sinful behaviour that was rife in these cities, and the fact that the people had turned against God. One thing in particular that was unacceptable to God was the incidence of homosexuality.

In Genesis chapter 18, from verse 16 on we read the full account of what happened and how the people in those cities tried to force their way into Lot's house to have sex with his male visitors.

What the Bible says

Many people are not even aware that rapes are recorded in the Bible; therefore, they are not able to understand how women in Biblical times managed, nor can they truly comprehend what occurred to them because of these horrific acts.

Generations go by, but women all over the world experience the same things over and over again. Sadly, one of those common occurrences is the suffering brought about by rape. The list seems almost endless. There is the helplessness that is felt after the attack has ended … the anger and fear that engulfs you and haunts your every move … the worry over whether you should seek help combined with the fear of what might happen to you as a result of telling. Then there is the fear that people will judge and condemn you, and all of this on top of the stain you cannot seem to wash away no matter how hard you try. You then find yourself suffering with lowered self-esteem, and you cannot seem to overcome it no matter how hard you try. There is the guilt you feel as you desperately go over the events in your mind, again and again, trying to work out what you could have done differently or how you may have brought this upon yourself

Your entire being is engulfed with desperation as you try to force yourself to put it all behind you and move on. You cope with the daily struggle of fighting to hang on to your self-worth and dignity as you face the world head on and prove that you are in fact better than the horrible atrocity that has been done to you.

Just Want to be Loved for Me...

There are many stories in the Bible that come to mind when discussing the topic of rape. These all bear testament to the fact that sadly, rape has been around for as long as human beings have walked the earth. Aside from the story about Lot mentioned above, there is another well-known story told in the book of Judges, chapter 19 about a Levite and his concubine.

It tells of how they travelled to another part of the country and stayed overnight in a stranger's house. Once they were settled in for the night, some men from the local village came beating on the door, demanding to be allowed to sleep with the man. There was no intention to seek permission from the Levite himself. This illustrates very clearly the depravity of the whole situation and the fact that these men were clearly not operating in the ways of God. The host, seeking in desperation to spare the Levite from being invaded in this evil way, offered his daughter, who was a virgin (even though she was also the Levite's concubine), to the men.

The village men were reluctantly appeased by this offer. However, the whole thing went horribly wrong when they badly abused the concubine throughout the entire night and then brought her battered and bruised body and left it outside their door. By the time the household knew she was there, she was already dead. Her hands were frozen in death, forever reaching upward in a last desperate effort to open the door. The Levite, in his grieving rage, cut the girl's body into pieces and sent a piece to each of the twelve tribes to show them the horror of what had been done to the girl. This had the effect of triggering a war to avenge her death.

There is another woman in the Bible whose story I want to concentrate on more deeply in talking about the subject of rape. Over the next few pages, I will break down the story of Dinah in a bid to explain the events that occurred and thereby fully share her story.

Dinah's story shows very clearly that the plight of women has been the same throughout the generations, and we share the same experiences irrespective of time or geographical constraints. If you have experienced the pain and trauma associated with rape, this chapter is definitely for you. It may even be that you are or have supported someone you know who is going through this.

Be encouraged in all things, and know that in the midst of experiencing trauma, pain and helplessness, God is standing by waiting for you to allow him into your life. He hurts for you too, and is distressed to see you, the precious work of his own creation, suffer pain.

However, as strange as it may seem, God actually needs your permission to act in your life. Once you let him in, he will gently cover you with his warmth, love and comfort.

He will bring peace to your troubled mind and he will hold your hand through the painful healing process. This is even when, in midst of it all, you are having a bad day and just feel like giving up, or when you feel like the healing or change is not happening fast enough and you can't hold on. You are definitely not alone no matter how much it feels like you are. He is there; you just need to reach out and ask him to take over. Then gently, step by step, he will lead you into the destiny he created you for originally. Only then will

Just Want to be Loved for Me...

you become the magnificent woman of purpose he created you to be.

If you want to ask God to be a part of your life now, or you want to ask him to help you in your situation, take a moment now and talk to him. He is waiting to hear from you because he loves you.

Dinah's story

The woman I want to tell you about is called Dinah. You will find her story in the book of Genesis chapter 34. Many people have not heard of her, as she is not one of the more popular women of the Bible. However, her story is still very important. She was the daughter of Jacob and Leah. Most people have heard a lot about her brothers, who eventually formed the twelve tribes of Israel, but Dinah was the only daughter born to Jacob.

Very little is known about Dinah or her life prior to this event, but we read that she lived with her family and her people on the Hebrew campsite. Her father had bought the parcel of land from the rulers, and he had pitched his tents there just outside the city. I can only imagine what it must have been like to be the only girl among twelve brothers. It is unlikely that she would have been able to join in with their everyday activities simply because she was a girl. The emphasis on her upbringing would have been to enable her to develop the skills she would need to be a good wife, mother and homemaker.

As for the boys, they would have been trained to take care of and manage the family assets. In their case, the main assets would have been the livestock and the land. They would have matured into good strong men able to provide and care for their families. As a part of the chosen nation of God, their upbringing would have included teaching them to follow the religious laws and to worship God according to his commandments.

Dinah would not have been party to any of this training because it never would have been her responsibility. When she was older and a married woman, these duties would be carried out by her husband.

I imagine that she was loved and spoilt by all her brothers. They probably teased her and played with her when they were all at home, and they most definitely would have been fiercely protective of her. Local boys who would have been interested in flirting with her or picking on her would rightly have been afraid of her twelve brothers, and so she would not have been the first choice to bully or flirt with.

She probably felt quite lonely and different in her family as the only girl, having no control over her life the way her brothers did theirs. She would have been unable to plan or set goals for her future, as this would all be the responsibility of the husband that would eventually be chosen for her. She would have known of this inequality in her status from a very early age. It is also likely that, not knowing there could be any different scenario for her life, she would have willingly accepted her fate.

Shechem sees Dinah

We are told in the Bible that one day, Dinah left the family's campsite to visit the other women in the city. We are not told the real purpose of her visit, or why she left the

Just Want to be Loved for Me...

protection of the family on her own. While she was there among the other women, she gradually became aware that someone was eyeing her with great interest. It was a very handsome and eligible young man called Shechem, and she was most flattered to realise that he was the king's son. The other women began to tease her and make jokes about how obvious she was in her attraction to him, and Dinah blushed with embarrassment and shyness.

She was still very young, and although she expected to get married at some stage, she had never really given it much thought. As the only girl in the family, she was much more of a tomboy and liked nothing better than to hang out with her brothers and play-fight with them. Even more enjoyable was when she teased them mercilessly and they chased her in feigned anger. When they caught her, they would tickle her until she screamed for mercy in between her laughter and giggling.

Her mother, on the other hand, always scolded her to behave in a more ladylike manner. Soon Dinah realised that it was time to put away her childish behaviour and behave in a more appropriate way. Her body had filled out and she had a very slender and alluring silhouette.

Dinah was a ravishing beauty, and everyone seemed to know it except her. She remained oblivious to her charm and the impact that her infectious laughter had on men. In fact, it was her purity and innocence that served to further enhance her overall attraction.

Shechem was a prince and therefore used to being surrounded by beauty and charm. It was no surprise that he should be attracted to Dinah. As a prince, he could have his pick of any woman he wanted. In return, any woman would gladly give herself, her daughter or all her possessions for the chance to be intimate with him. Women knew that he would be king one day, and that having him as a husband or lover would greatly enhance their status. Yet all these lovely women were diminished in his sight after he set eyes on Dinah, and he stopped noticing them all.

He found himself thinking about Dinah all the time. He was deeply attracted to her because she was so different. She was a stranger in the land, and although he did not actually know her people very well, he had often heard stories about them and their invisible God. This was the same God who had led them victoriously from one battle to the next. It was a rather quaint concept really, and one he did not understand, although he was curious about it.

On that fateful day, he had heard that Dinah had come to visit the women again. He found himself arranging to go past the place where they regularly sat together and chatted. He had originally intended to go by casually just to look at her one more time. He was driven by an innate desire to see the face that haunted his dreams and made his heart ache. He found himself asking many questions about her after each of her visits. He fought hard to keep his questions non-committal and casual. Shechem was ashamed of his feelings and afraid of what people would think if they knew that he was smitten with Dinah.

He was unable to explain it reasonably, no matter how hard he tried. He was no novice to matters of the heart and had been able to have ample practice to perfect his technique and sexual abilities. No woman would dare to refuse him as the king's son. Yet here he was feeling insecure and not

Just Want to be Loved for Me...

quite knowing how to approach Dinah with what he felt in his heart. He also was in an awkward position in that he had never felt so deeply for a woman before, especially one he had never spoken to. It made him uncomfortable and he was annoyed to realise that he was not in control of his feelings.

In a weak bid to erase her from his mind, he had ordered all his favourites to be brought to him from the harem at the palace. Yet none of the women were able to distract him for long enough. In the midst of their lovemaking, he would find himself avidly fantasising that he was holding Dinah. He imagined himself kissing her tenderly and taking great delight as she shyly surrendered her all to him. In his mind, he could almost smell the erotic scent of her perfume as he buried his face in her long wavy hair. He imagined himself dropping soft feathery kisses all over her, and he could almost feel the soft silkiness of her skin as he stroked it and ran his fingers over it.

Today when he saw her, he felt a familiar rush of emotion course over his entire being. She was just as beautiful in real life as he had imagined her a hundred times before. He knew that this had to be the day when he took matters into his own hands. He intended to talk to her so that he could determine whether she found him attractive too. Then he could assess how to approach her family to ask for her hand in marriage. He knew they had different rules about everything, so he needed to make sure that he would not cause offence. He approached her and asked her to come with him to talk.

Dinah paused for a moment, not quite sure what to do or how to approach this situation. She was suddenly dumbstruck and frantically tried to assess the situation in her mind. It would be very difficult to refuse to go with him; after all, he was the prince. Yet she had never been alone with any man before and was not sure it was appropriate to do so now. She knew exactly what her mother would say, and yet she did not feel confident enough to offend the prince in the midst of his people and on his land. She was sure that if she did refuse him, it would have dire consequences for her and for her family as well when they found out. They would also have to bear the brunt of any repercussions that might result from the king's anger. She was in a very tricky situation and she knew it.

By now, the other women were giving each other knowing looks, and some of them were even envious that Dinah should be chosen to receive favour from the prince instead of them. They encouraged her to go to him, and reassured her that she would be fine. It would be a shame to miss an opportunity like this, and there was no guarantee that it would ever come again. Dinah decided to go peacefully with Shechem. The truth was that she found him attractive too, but being a proper lady, she never would have let on to the others the depth of her feelings. Anyway, there was no harm in talking together, and who knows what may come of it.

Once Shechem is alone with Dinah, his emotions go into overdrive and his passion, longing and anxiety about the whole situation get the better of him. He is angry about the lack of control he senses within himself and hates the effect she has on him. He decides that maybe if he can have her just once he will then be able to move on with his life. The impact of her charms will be reduced, he reasons, and the unrequited love he feels for her will be salved somewhat.

Just Want to be Loved for Me...

Shechem makes the fateful mistake of listening to what this feeling is telling him. He reaches for her gently at first, but he is shocked to find that she flinches away from him in fear. Her beautiful smiling face becomes disfigured by fear and trepidation. Her beautiful almond shaped eyes well up with tears that spill over onto her perfectly formed cheekbones as she pleads with him to stop. Shechem can't believe what is happening; this is so different from the fantasy he has created in his mind, the one where she succumbs to his charm and is pliable to his will. This feeling of being somehow betrayed by her (because he was so certain she would surrender and melt in his arms) makes him angry all over again, and he reaches for her more roughly this time, determined to show her who she is daring to reject. Drawing her to him, he presses his hard masculine body against her soft skin. He knows full well that she does not have the physical strength to fight him off or even to stop him. He takes her forcefully, paying no attention to her cries for him to stop.

She is in a very vulnerable position indeed and is away from the protection of her family and community. The most telling fact of all is that the attacker is actually a prince of the land. It would be hard for a young girl in her position to have the confidence or strength to stand up to an important man like Shechem. She hurts all over, especially on her arms and places on her body where his fingers gripped her hard to force her to hold still. She had given up fighting him after a while and had lain as still and limp as she could under his touch. Having now seen this most evil and aggressive side to his nature, she is afraid to aggravate him more than she has already done. She has no way of knowing the extent of his cruelty, and whether or not she will even be allowed to live to see the end of this awful ordeal. In many ways, she knows that she is already as good as dead. This event will have a completely life-changing impact on her life.

It is hard to understand exactly what was going on in Shechem's mind and why he chose to take this dangerous course of action. One may ask why he chose to rape Dinah without regard for what it would do to her or to her family. Given the position of women in that time, he would have known that she would never be able to be married afterwards and that her life could only follow a certain path marred by the shame and disgrace she would endure. She would be robbed of being a wife and mother. She would only be sought after by men who would see her as a quick thrill and nothing more.

Because Dinah was a daughter of Jacob, with twelve brothers in her family and many other relatives, Shechem's actions could have easily led to war between his people and hers. Yet he was driven by a lustful desire to have her without due regard for the consequences. His actions seem completely irrational and defy explanation. He was clearly thinking with regard to his physical needs and not with any measure of good sense.

As soon as his physical needs are sated, he is consumed with guilt and fear, and his rational being takes over. As he lies there spent on top of her, he remembers how much he had loved her from afar. Now that he has committed this unthinkable act, he is unsure how it will all pan out.

As Dinah remains still and lifeless beneath him, he knows that he has hurt her both physically and spiritually. In sympathy and love, he reaches to stroke her hair and face and is again jolted back to reality when she recoils in

Just Want to be Loved for Me...

horror. She instinctively fears the worst: that he is about to repeat the physical assault on her already ravaged body. This makes Shechem even sadder than before. It is very painful for him to realise that the young woman who consumed so much of his thoughts and desires cannot bear to be touched by him.

Upon reflection, he begins to recall how much he cares for her, and realises with a start that she is his dream girl. More importantly, Dinah is indeed a very lovable and attractive girl. He is beginning to look at her as a real person for the first time, especially now that he is no longer driven by his insatiable need to have her and possess her.

Now in the cold light of day he is no longer consumed by her beauty or her physically young and sexy body. He can now see her positive attributes as a person and can rationally take into account who she is and how influential her family is. This makes him feel even worse than he already does. In addition to all of this, he now realises that he has closely bonded with Dinah during their physical encounter. No other woman has ever had that effect on him, and it scares him.

Love is in the air

Shechem now deeply regrets what he has done and he wants to make it right. He accepts that he loves Dinah very much and wants her to be his wife. He is convinced that no other woman could ever take her place and that she is his soul mate. He is also aware that this decision to do the right thing could also save a potentially volatile situation from getting worse. Marrying Dinah would also allow him to at least try to right a very obvious wrong.

Shechem begins to speak kindly to Dinah to get her on his side. It is very important to him that she agree with his next plan. He is in effect holding out an olive branch to make peace with her. As a woman, she would be redeemed and would not have to suffer a life of being regarded as spoilt goods. We are not told what her response was, but we do know that she did not return home to her family. She stays in Shechem's house to wait it out and to hear what her fate will be.

She would have been only too aware of the options before her. Neither was ideal; she would either be sent home where she would live out her days unmarried, a disgraced woman, or she would spend her life married to a man whose first intimate act toward her had been one of violence, subjection and violation. She ponders everything over and over again, and sadly accepts that as a woman with no rights, the ultimate choice will never be hers anyway. She will have to accept whatever fate throws her way and live with it.

Shechem is so disturbed by the whole event that he reluctantly confides in Hamor, his father and the king. He leaves nothing out and actually tells him the whole story. He concludes his account by telling his father that he wants to right the wrong he has done to Dinah by marrying her. There is, however, the small matter of her family to consult. Had this been a woman from his own land, the king could have ordered it to be so and that would have been an end to it. However, Shechem knows that the Hebrew people are governed by different rules. He feels totally out of his depth and is unable to handle this alone. He begs Hamor, his father to support him by conducting the necessary negotiations with her family to make it happen.

Just Want to be Loved for Me...

The story doesn't go into much detail about Hamor's response to his son's actions. One can imagine that he might have been filled with mixed emotions, the strongest of which was probably fury at his son's reckless act of violence. As a prince, he had the pick of any girl in his land, and at some point, he would be matched up with a girl who was worthy of his social standing and fit to bear the next king.

Hamor reluctantly agrees to accompany his son to speak to Dinah's family and secure their agreement for the marriage. It never occurred to Shechem that Dinah's family could refuse to allow him to marry her, especially given who he was and also the fate that would surely befall Dinah if they refused.

Shechem and Hamor set out together to see Dinah's family to sort things out.

Jacob finds out

When Jacob finds out that Dinah, his little girl, has been raped and defiled, he is filled with anger and dismay. His mind races with a thousand questions at once. He wants to know how such a thing could have happened to his baby, yet he knows he would be sickened and revolted to hear about it, as every word would conjure up painful images of the assault on his daughter. He is wracked with guilt and wonders, *How did we fail Dinah as a family? Furthermore, how did she manage to wander so far out from the protection of the family?*

Jacob is a smart man, and despite his distress at being given this news, he keeps his peace until his sons, Dinah's brothers, come back from the field. He is already looking at the bigger picture. This is a momentous event, one that could possibly lead to very serious consequences involving war and death. Politically things were very fickle in that region, and so it was important for Jacob to weigh the options carefully.

The perpetrator is the son of the local king and has the power and connections to wage a war against them with their allies. Jacob knows that whatever he does now could potentially affect the whole of his people who live outside the city in their tents. As a leader, he would not speak out of turn rashly and emotionally. Whilst waiting for his sons to come back he has the chance to go over things in his mind in order to come up with a reasoned response.

As one would expect, when the sons come home and are told the news, they are also very angry and outraged. They feel incapable of believing this horrendous thing has happened to their sister. Some of them greet the news with sadness and shock, others with anger and aggression. Their father Jacob has been put into a very sticky situation where he will be forced to keep order among the brethren until they are able to think clearly and decide what to do. This is despite the fact that as a father he wants to avenge Dinah's honour and reach out to console his baby girl, all at the same time. Yet he has to be the voice of reason even though he feels so far from reasonable inside. He has to stay calm and show leadership even when his mind feels like it has been scrambled by the shock of the news.

Dinah's mother and the other women are withdrawn and quiet, their eyes red and puffy from the constant crying and distress this has caused them all. They grieve for the

Just Want to be Loved for Me...

loss of Dinah's future and the pain she will have to endure. They also mourn the fact that they have not been able to see her or to comfort her and for their own helplessness in this situation. As women, they understand the shame and humiliation she must feel at this time. They console themselves with the knowledge that there will be time to support her once it has all been settled.

The family's reaction is no less than Hamor had expected, and he tries his best to console and appease them. He reassures them that his son Shechem is very sorry and that he now loves Dinah and wants her to be his wife. This appears to be a good solution, as it will be difficult to find a husband for Dinah now that she has been raped.

Hamor wants to use this opportunity for them all to have a closer relationship with each other. A marriage between Shechem and Dinah would join them all together as one people. They would live, work and play together and develop a united purpose. This would create a sense of permanence for Jacob and his people and they would be able to live and trade freely.

Hamor urges Jacob to accept his offer and to reach a peaceable solution. As a leader, he too is concerned about the effect it could have if they were to go to war against Jacob and his people. He wants to avoid this consequence at all costs.

The solution to the problem

Hamor continues to plead with them, and to sweeten the deal, he offers to pay whatever dowry they ask for. In addition, he will give whatever gifts they want if only they will agree to the marriage. Hamor's position is clear, and it is now over to Jacob and his family to make their move.

A plan is hatched by Dinah's family in a bid to buy time and to get out of a potentially volatile situation. The family tells Hamor that there is no way they can give Dinah to be Shechem's wife. This is because Hamor and his people are a nation of uncircumcised men, and this would be a reproach to Jacob's people because of their religious laws and customs. It was totally unacceptable and out of the question.

This refers back to Genesis chapter 17 when God spoke to Abraham and established a covenant between him and his people. All males must be circumcised eight days after they are born as a sign of the covenant. If outsiders are brought into the people, they too should be circumcised and bear the sign of the covenant. The law is clear: if any male does not get circumcised, he should be cut off from the people.

This very nearly happened to the sons of Moses in Exodus 4:25. After God told Moses to go back to Egypt, Moses obeyed and brought his family with him. One night as they rested at an inn along the way, the Lord came to kill Moses' son, because although he was an heir to the covenant, he had never been circumcised. This is because Moses had moved away from his people and had not followed the old laws. He had instead adapted his life to the laws of the land he now lived in. Zipporah, Moses' wife, understood very quickly why the Lord sought to kill (or cut off) her son, and she quickly took a sharp stone and cut off the foreskin of her son and threw it at his feet. The boy was thankfully saved to continue the journey with Moses and Zipporah.

Just Want to be Loved for Me...

Coming back to the story of Dinah's fate, Jacob tells Hamor that if he will agree for all the males from his people to be circumcised in line with their religious laws, then the two groups of people can freely become one people when Shechem and Dinah are joined together in marriage. Jacob then gives an ultimatum: If Hamor will not agree to this, then Jacob and his family will take Dinah with them and leave the land completely.

This is a big thing for Jacob to ask, and it probably seems unlikely that Hamor and Shechem will agree to such a thing. It provides a good way for Jacob to get out of a tricky situation without causing the outbreak of war.

However, the newfound love that burns within Shechem for Dinah leads him to readily agree to Jacob's demands, and he is so keen to redeem himself that he immediately goes and gets circumcised to be an example to the others.

He then joins his father in convincing the other men of the benefits of following suit and getting circumcised as well. They offer the men the promise of a larger people, more women they can take as wives as well as more opportunities for trade, business relationships and assets. After all, they reason, the land itself is large enough for them all to share without causing a strain.

Their enthusiasm to redeem the wrong committed against Dinah coupled with the very clear benefits of joining both sets of people paid off. Everyone agreed to the terms. In any event, how could they refuse a direct command from their king, especially when it meant so much to him? So all the men agreed and they were all circumcised in accordance with the agreement. This would have had the effect of bringing them in line with the religious requirements, thus putting them under the covering of the Abrahamic covenant, finally making them one people who were able to move on and put the unpleasant past firmly behind them.

Dinah waits

We have no way of knowing how Dinah was coping during all these negotiations. What was going through her mind? We *do* know that she did not return home, but instead was still in Shechem's home awaiting the decision. I am sure that inside she felt emotionally and spiritually numbed to all that had taken place. The events must have played over and over in her mind, causing her to be unable to block the images that forced their way into her consciousness. Even at night, they dominated her dreams.

Her emotions went from completely hating and blaming Shechem in one instant for his act of total cruelty against her, and completely blaming herself in the next. She analysed and assessed her every movement to see how she could have behaved differently and what part she had played in causing this. She had always been so loved and adored by everyone, and she could not bear the thought that she would now be a marked woman. Other women would now use her as an example of how *not* to be. Even now that it was all over, she could still feel the rough sensation of his forceful hands on her body. She remembered the innate sense of panic, fright and helplessness that she had felt in those terrifying moments. She had realised how powerless she was in the situation. She had often heard that time is a healer. However, in her present state of mind, she could not imagine a time when things would ever be alright again.

Just Want to be Loved for Me...

To Dinah, it seems there will be no happy ending for her, despite which way the decision made among the men would go. She contemplates the predicament she faces. She could end up being married to a man with whom her first contact was a forcible and physical rape. How would this affect her ability to trust this man to become the head of her life, the provider of her household and the father to her children? How could she become as one flesh with him in future sexual unions when there would obviously be the element of fear and terror present? Each sexual act would be a painful reminder of how she was treated. She would always be reminded that the sacred and beautiful act that every woman looks forward to as a mark of her womanhood has been used as a weapon of domineering force and pain against her own body.

If, on the other hand, her family did not accept the offer of marriage, then she would be a defiled woman and would probably remain single and childless. This event would leave a mark of condemnation and shame, which everyone would know about, and they would know that she had been forcibly violated in the most sacred parts of her body. She would be judged continuously, never able to fulfil her purpose or destiny as a woman, wife, or mother. She was in a no-win situation and worse still, she felt totally helpless and frustrated at the thought that the decision would be made by the men in her life, and she would never be consulted as to her feelings on the matter.

She longed for the comfort of her mother's embrace and her words of wisdom. She always knew what to say or do if there was a crisis. Dinah had always been able to rely on her mother completely. This time such reliance was not possible because no matter how much she hurt for her daughter, Leah could have no say in the matter, either. Dinah knew there were no words to salve the pain she was feeling. Nothing could wash away the feeling of shame and humiliation that refused to leave her no matter how hard she tried. She was comforted only by the fact that her family were always there for her through all things.

Yet she knew this was a road she had to face alone. She could not bear to see the pain or sorrow that would reflect itself in her mother's eyes. Dinah hurt to think that she had caused it. She was afraid to see her brothers and worse still, her father. They all adored her, and she was humiliated that they would know what had happened to her. If this whole sorry affair caused a war, it would be because of her. Worse still, if any of them died or were injured as a result of what happened to her, she knew she could never forgive herself.

Dinah knew that she needed this time to pull herself together so that when she had to face her family, she would be able to do so from a position of strength. She was consumed by an overwhelming need to be strong for their sakes.

Right now, she needed to be alone to prepare herself for whatever decision would be made. She tries in vain to banish the memories from her mind and asks herself the question of why this had to happen to HER over and over again. She tries to find comfort by praying but could not find the words. Every new attempt brings a fresh wave of bitter tears and pain from her broken spirit. The words are hijacked by the involuntary sobs that rack her bruised body as she bravely tries to control the situation.

The aftermath

This act of compliance by Shechem and his people should have been a happy ending to a very sad story. However, what would happen next would change the course of events forever. I do not think it ever occurred to Jacob and his sons that Hamor and Shechem would actually agree to their terms. They were now faced with a dilemma about what to do next.

At this rate, Shechem was about to become their in-law, and for all intents and purposes, this would mean he had gotten away with raping Dinah. He would have gone totally unpunished. There was still a lot of anger in her family about what he had done, and they had still not been able to see their sister to make sure that she was alright.

Before anything else could be decided as a family, two of Dinah's brothers, Simeon and Levi, took it upon themselves to avenge their sister. They were definitely not appeased by the mockery of the agreement that was being made between the families. Such an easy settlement could never make the situation right. They were consumed with anger and hurt over the plight of the sister and would never agree to give her to someone who had used force as a weapon to get her as a wife. They had very strong emotions of anger and revenge mingled with guilt that they had failed to protect their sister. Furthermore, they were appalled that their father had not taken a stronger line. The way Simeon and Levi saw it, Shechem had treated their sister as though she was a whore, and no amount of backtracking now would change that fact.

They waited until three days had passed after Hamor's men had been circumcised according to the agreement so it would seem as though all was going according to plan. Their anger and thirst for vengeance was picking up momentum by the hour. By now, Hamor's men would be in great pain from the circumcision and would be at their lowest point as they waited for their bodies to heal. Levi and Simeon chose this exact point to effect their revenge. Driven by their rage, they armed themselves with swords and boldly went to the city and attacked and killed all the men. They met very little resistance from the men. They also killed Shechem and Hamor, and they took their sister Dinah from Hamor's house and brought her home. They also raided the city and took their livestock, wealth, wives and children.

What a dramatic end to the story. Jacob, however, was very upset that Simeon and Levi had done this, and he became very worried that the other tribes nearby would hear of what had happened, form alliances and come to attack them. As a man of peace, he wanted to maintain the good relationships he had established with the neighbouring tribes. However, Simeon and Levi refused to be reasoned with and remained completely unrepentant. They fully stood by their actions as warriors defending their own. They had sent a very clear message to everyone about what would happen if people messed about with them or sought to disrespect their family again. They had done right by the family and were not going to be made to feel guilty about it. The story ends in Genesis chapter 34, verse 31 with them challenging their father by asking, "Should he treat our sister like a harlot?"

This is the last we hear of Dinah, and then she disappears from the Biblical records. We never get to find out if she

Just Want to be Loved for Me...

has a happy ending. Was she able to move on from this traumatic event and fulfil her destiny? Or was this event designed to be her main contribution to history, or even to the destiny of the line that would eventually bring forth a Messiah that would save people from their sins?

This event, however, would greatly affect and change things for Simeon and Levi in the future. Their father, Jacob, would eventually leave behind two legacies: one to do with the family wealth and the other to do with kingship rights. These were both usually passed on to the eldest son. In this case, that should have been Reuben. However, Jacob decides against this because he knows that Reuben disrespected him and had an affair with Bilhah, who was the mother of Jacob's sons Dan and Naptali. In Genesis chapter 49, Jacob described Reuben as 'unstable as water' because he had defiled his father's bed.

The next two down the line to inherit are Simeon and Levi, but Jacob feels unable to allow them to inherit it either. This is because of the judgement call they made to avenge Dinah's honour. Jacob curses their anger and calls it an act of cruelty because he thinks they went too far. He remembers that a whole kingdom was destroyed by them for the single crime against their sister.

The fourth son in line is Judah, who is so far down the line that no one would have ever expected him to be the one to inherit the kingship right. However, Jacob blesses him and gives him that inheritance. Therefore, the Messiah would eventually come from the line of Judah, not from any one of Judah's three older brothers. Their own choices, and their ultimate behaviour based on those choices, caused them to lose their birthrights. The other right, which had to do with family wealth, was passed on to Joseph, who was also one of the youngest of the brothers.

What about Dinah?

This story probably has a deep impact on your heart if you have also been the victim of rape or molestation. On the face of it, it may seem that you have more choices than Dinah had, simply because we live in modern times, but the consequences of those choices may have the same impact on you as they did on her.

You may choose to tell and endure the shame and humiliation of having to relate intimate details of the event to strangers. You may have to endure embarrassing medical examinations or even damning accusations from a defence lawyer whose only interest is to secure the release of their client. This is all in addition to the personal suffering you will face as your family, friends and colleagues learn what you have been through.

If you choose not to tell, you force yourself into a world of silence where you lock away your emotions, feelings, fear and suffering. Many do in fact choose this option, unwilling to confront what has happened head on, falsely thinking that it is easier to forget and move on, but this never proves to be the easiest way because you never really forget. This locking away and not wanting to address the emotional hurt and trauma will lead to other difficulties and affect your ability to relate to people throughout your life.

You will never feel completely whole again and may even adopt a permanent mask of happiness to show the world. This will never reveal the fragile little person inside struggling to

Just Want to be Loved for Me...

put the past firmly behind her. The unhappiness and the emotional vacuum inside of you will haunt you again and again when you are alone or are beset by doubt, fear, and low self-esteem.

Many rape victims find themselves searching endlessly for something to fill that vacuum, desperately looking for ways to bring comfort to themselves. This can often be through excessive amounts of food, alcohol, work and/or shopping. Some people fill all the available time in their lives being everything to everyone else, leaving no time to fill their own needs or even to know what those needs are. They keep themselves so busy that they do not even have time to think, and at the end of the day, they are so tired that they fall into bed at night in a state of complete exhaustion.

Life is not fair, and we never know what we are going to face as we go along. I would imagine that Dinah was only able to make peace with her situation through a renewed relationship with God. Who else could help her to come to terms with herself about what happened? He would have become her healer, her provider and finally, her Prince of peace.

She must have finally surrendered her life and her all to him in the full knowledge that she was not able to control the madness that sought to engulf her and rob her of her future. She would have come to the realisation that only God could turn this hopeless situation around. She would have looked in all directions to find the answers, first looking into her past after having found none in the present, or by trying to manipulate the future herself. When she looked to the past, she would have found Yahweh, or Jehovah the God of Abraham, Isaac and Jacob, her father. Now he would be ***her***

God, and she herself would claim the promises of blessing and prosperity that had been handed down to her people through the generations.

God must have heard and welcomed her call and was only too willing to be all that she needed him to be and more. Only then would she have been able to find peace and move into the destiny he created her for even before the world began.

If you are like Dinah, whether you have chosen to tell anyone about your ordeal or not, I want you to know that true healing and inner peace will only come from God. You may wonder where God was when the event took place, and why it seems like he has been so distant from you at times; you may have even wondered if he really loves you.

We are not able to understand everything that happens to us, but I do know for sure that he is waiting for you to ask him for help in turning this situation around, and not just as a one-off favour. No, it is much better than that; he actually wants you to have a relationship with him.

You can get to know him by talking to him, reading his words in the Bible, and talking to and being with other people who know him and love him and who care for you, such as people in your local church.

Once you start getting to know God on a personal basis, you will understand things more clearly and will be able to see the things he likes and dislikes. You can also find out about his personality by listening to the testimony of other people as they tell how God has worked in their lives. You can also know God's heart by how he reacts to people in the

Just Want to be Loved for Me...

Bible stories. The good thing is that he doesn't change and always stays the same. Therefore, you can have confidence and faith in what you learn of him, and you can begin to allow him to work in your life just as he has worked in the lives of so many others.

If you have been holding on to issues in your life because you have not found a way to let go, try God today. Be like Dinah – ask God to release you from the heavy load you have been carrying, then simply let go and let him take control of your life. You have nothing to lose and everything to gain by trying this. Go on … take the first step … talk to him. He's ready to listen and to speak to your heart in return.

Chapter Three

Incest

Tamar's Story

Introduction

Another person in the Bible who experienced the ordeal of rape is a woman called Tamar. When I began studying her story, it was interesting to find that very few people know about her and fewer still know her story. In fact, in trying to research this on the Internet, I was only able to find lots of information on another Biblical woman with the same name of Tamar. That woman ended up being a direct ancestor to Jesus in the family line of Judah. She would have made an excellent study as well, as she too suffered great adversity at the hands of others and ended up triumphant in her situation. You can read about that Tamar's story in the book of Genesis chapter 39 from verse 6 to verse 20.

The Tamar I would like to discuss in this chapter was one of King David's daughters. Many people have associated her story with the subject of incest. For reference purposes, you can read her story in 2 Samuel chapter 13. Although she had many other siblings, Tamar's story seems to focus on her relationship with her two brothers called Absalom and Ammon.

Incest is an abuse of both opportunity and trust in an illicit sexual relationship or molestation between immediate family members. This abuse may be combined with fear, mental or physical abuse and is often craftily bound in the utmost secrecy and intimidation.

Ammon falls in love

Ammon is the first of King David's sons, and his mother was a different woman from the mother that both Tamar and her brother Absalom share. This in effect makes Ammon their half brother.

We are not told anything about Tamar before this time, and the story opens up in chapter 13 with Ammon declaring his intense love for his half sister. Having watched her grow up from childhood into a beautiful young lady, he finds himself thinking about her all the time. He notices everything about her, from her beautiful face with her radiant smile right down to her young nubile body, which is subtly outlined beneath her flowing robes. He knows every feature of her face by heart and has memorised its beauty thoroughly. It is the last thing he sees at night in his mind's eye before he finally drops off to sleep and the first thing he thinks about the moment he wakes up in the morning.

He knows there is no future in pursuing his thoughts, but they are always there haunting him and filling his every free moment nonetheless. He worries incessantly about his attraction to Tamar. Somewhere deep within him he knows that this is a forbidden relationship and that he should stop, but he finds it almost impossible to do so. Intermittently he allows his thoughts to wander randomly, and he fantasises that it has all been worked out: He sees her as his wife, and she loves him passionately just as he loves her. At other times, he imagines that the two of them making love in a special way that only they could ever do. In between all of this, he is racked with feelings of guilt and remorse, to the point that he actually begins to feel physically sick and depraved. Tamar is such a gentle, sweet natured and innocent girl, and he feels like a monster for even thinking such things about her.

Ammon's situation is made worse by the fact that not only is Tamar beautiful to look at, she is also a virgin, which makes it even more improper for Ammon to do anything

Just Want to be Loved for Me...

about his feelings. Having known her for all of her life, he is also in love with the person she is. She is popular and has a fantastic sense of humour. When Tamar was younger, Ammon used to love to watch as she laughed with her friends and teased them as they played together. Now that she is older, she has become more demure and serious in public. However, those who know her well also know that just below the surface she is still the same person she has always been and is just as much fun as ever. Instead of endearing him to her in a brotherly way, all of this excited him further and heightened his already raging hormones to a new level.

Ammon begins to feel very miserable indeed. He makes several futile attempts to show interest in the other pretty women around. There is a huge selection of young women to choose from. After all, he is the king's son and therefore any of the women would be happy to be favoured by his advances. However, he finds that he is unable to get his mind off Tamar, and therefore none of the other girls are acceptable to him. He finds himself selfishly comparing them all to Tamar. Of course, none of them are good enough and could never match her qualities.

Ammon becomes increasingly depressed, and this greatly affects his appetite and his ability to rouse himself to carry on with his duties. He is also very ashamed of himself and his thoughts, and he cannot trust himself to speak about it. Each time he sees Tamar, he feels a strange sense of awkwardness. He also feels tongue-tied, and his ears burn furiously whenever he blushes. Something has to be done to release him from this constant and daily pressure. He just cannot go on this way.

Friendship

If you have ever been warned about what may happen to you if you end up in the wrong company of friends, you have been given good advice and should listen to it carefully and take the advice seriously. Friends are a wonderful asset for anyone to have. They are there to share the good times and the bad with you. They are the ones who will not be afraid to break bad news to you or to tell you when you are wrong. Just because they may disagree with you on a particular issue does not mean that they hate you or that they will not be the first ones to help you if something else goes wrong.

Friends can have a greater influence on you than all of the other authority figures in your life. This can include your parents, family members, school authorities, your supervisor at work or even the law. This is wonderful when things are going well. However, this can all go wrong if the friends you have are not genuine or if they are not totally committed to your well being. Sometimes you may find yourself unsure or depressed. It is during these times when you might seek them out and rely on them to see you through. Their support is crucial in providing a voice of reason when you are unable to hear your own. Their advice or support can lead you to destruction, however, if you are not smart enough to see what is unfolding as a result.

Unfortunately, this is what happened to Ammon. He has a friend called Jonadab who thinks he is being a good friend by giving Ammon some advice and lots of encouragement to follow through on it. Jonadab is a very crafty friend, and he begins by teasing Ammon. He has noticed that Ammon seems very quiet and withdrawn lately. In addition, Ammon also seems to be getting thinner and has no appetite for

Just Want to be Loved for Me...

his food. Jonadab very quickly realises that something is wrong. He also knows that Ammon is a bit of a stubborn character. If Jonadab goes about asking him in the wrong way, Ammon will never tell him what is bothering him. So Jonadab takes the subtle approach first. He starts off by teasing Ammon that it is unacceptable for the king's prized son to be so thin.

However, this seems to make Ammon even more upset and withdrawn. Jonadab knows him really well, and he realises that whatever is making Ammon sad is more serious than he had first thought. He needs to find another way to get his friend to talk. After much cajoling and persistence on Jonadab's part, Ammon is worn down and eventually caves in. He tells Jonadab all about his distress and discomfort around Tamar. Once he starts to talk, he is so relieved to be able to share his problem that he finally tells his friend everything. Ammon confesses how much he desperately loves Tamar and how impossible it all is because she is his half sister. By this stage, Ammon cannot decide what to do about his feelings for Tamar, and he feels as though he is losing his mind over it.

Being Ammon's good friend, this would have been the perfect time for Jonadab to make a difference and offer Ammon some good counsel. Having confessed everything, Ammon needs Jonadab's support and advice very badly. He has gone over the situation in his mind repeatedly. He is no longer able to rationalise any kind of reasonable solution. However, he is sadly mistaken in thinking that his most trusted friend can help him. Even today, it is common for friends to cause perfectly reasonable people to go astray. Whilst it is good to have friends, we are reminded that when we are in trouble, we should first look to God. He alone has the solution we need. Through the Holy Spirit, he will show you what is right for you. Whatever he speaks to your heart will be confidential and non-judgemental.

Ammon appears to have bypassed the option of seeking God's counsel, and has got himself into a state. Instead of looking up for the answer, he is 'on the phone' to his friend.

This revelation is all that Jonadab needs to begin hatching a cruel and shameful plot. Instead of helping to find a way for Ammon to finally get this problem out of his head, he conjures up an elaborate plan and encourages Ammon to follow it through. This plan will pave the way for Ammon to be alone with his true love Tamar and to deal with the situation.

Jonadab tells Ammon to lie down on his bed and pretend to be extremely ill. Then he convinces Ammon that later on, when his father, King David, comes along to see him, he will be upset to see Ammon looking so ill and so weak. Ammon should seize this opportunity to ask his father, in his faintest voice, to allow his sister Tamar to come and give him some food to strengthen him. In particular, Jonadab tells Ammon to request that Tamar is to prepare the food in front of Ammon. This will give him some time to be alone with her.

Jonadab tells him that after this, Ammon can finally deal with Tamar and the situation. He tempts Ammon by suggesting that once Ammon tells her how he feels, who knows – she may even feel the same way. If not, Ammon will have her right where he can convince her. Remember, Jonadab suggests slyly, there will be no one around, and

Just Want to be Loved for Me...

you will have all the time you need to work on her until she agrees with you.

In Psalm chapter 1, we read that 'blessed is the man who walks not in the counsel of the ungodly...' This does not mean simply staying away from the places where 'sinners' congregate. Sadly, this is the way that some Christians choose to interpret it, but in doing so, they miss many opportunities to minister to someone who may really need to know about the goodness of God. After all, aren't we all sinners who are saved by the grace of God alone? When Christians minister only to people who are attending church already or are even just visiting the church, they are dealing with people who are already halfway there. Whilst this work is also important, it is often in places where 'sinners hang out' that the greatest need exists.

In this first chapter of Psalms, we are actually being warned not to take advice or counsel from the ungodly. If someone is not walking with God, he or she is unlikely to give you godly or 'wise' advice. In this case, the advice that Ammon gets from his 'friend' is definitely not wise counsel, and will lead him to act in a way that is definitely not within the laws of God.

The plot thickens

By the time that Jonadab is finished convincing Ammon that this plot will work, Ammon is fully confident and committed to carrying it out. Ammon sets the plan in motion almost immediately. He follows the agreed-upon instructions the letter. Sure enough, when his father, King David, sees how ill he is, there is no way he can refuse Ammon's simple request to have Tamar bring him some food and prepare it for him. *The boy seems so ill*, David must have thought, *even though I don't understand how he could have become so ill so quickly*. Nevertheless, David sees it as a positive sign that Ammon wants to eat something. At least this will go towards restoring his strength a little so that his frail body can fight off the sickness.

David thought back over the last few weeks and wondered whether he could have missed something. He remembered thinking that Ammon was getting a little bit thinner and that he seemed to have gone off his food. However, he had dismissed it as quickly as it had occurred to him. As the king, he had so many other things on his mind and a whole load of responsibilities that weighed him down like a ton of bricks. He mentally resolved to keep an eye on the situation. Because he was a loving father, it always destabilised David when any of his children were not well or were unhappy.

David immediately goes to see Tamar. She is the darling apple of his eye and touches his heart in a way that no male child ever could. Her beautiful face is only surpassed by her warm, sweet nature. She is definitely a miniature of her mother, and David is reminded of how much he loves them both. He remembers when Tamar was born and how tiny she was when cupped between his large hands. He had examined her carefully, unable to believe the miracle that God had given him. As a little girl, she sought him out whenever she could. He had delighted in her sweetness, her innocence and her adoration of him. Unlike many other people, she loved him simply because he was her daddy, not because he was the king. His heart melted with affection every time he saw her, and he would do anything for her. He knew without a doubt that he would protect her with his own life if he needed to.

Just Want to be Loved for Me...

On that day, there were other pressing things on his mind; he needs to take care of his son Ammon, whom he also loves and who is ill. David tells Tamar what she needs to do and sends her to Ammon's house to prepare food for him. Tamar, being a faithful daughter and sister, is duty bound to obey her father's command to care for her sick brother. When she goes to Ammon's house, she is upset to see that he does indeed seem to be very ill.

She is less convinced, though, that she is the only one who can prepare the food for him. There were so many servants and helpers around, and several other relatives as well. It did cross her mind, though, that maybe she had been asked because of the trust factor. Helpers were fine for seeing to the washing and keeping the house clean. However, when it came to cooking, it could be risky to use someone outside the trusted family circle. It was common for servants to plot against their masters and attempt to poison them.

Ammon, being the eldest child, would eventually take David's place. This would most definitely make him a target. As Tamar ponders this eventuality, she stops short in her thoughts and wonders if this recent sickness is the result of someone's attempt to hurt her brother. She realises he has been looking pale and withdrawn recently, but she has not paid it much attention until now.

Anyway, whatever the reason for Ammon's rather unusual request, she is committed to fulfilling it, as doing so also means doing as her father has asked, and she always respects her father's wishes. She begins to prepare the food, chatting to Ammon as she works. She kneads the dough and prepares the cakes in the next room.

Dangerous liaisons

It is at this point that everything begins to go horribly wrong. Ammon knows he intends to follow the bad advice of his friend and take advantage of an innocent situation with his own sister, no less. He pushes from his mind any traces of guilt that try to warn him, and he orders everyone to leave the room. When he and Tamar are completely alone, he asks Tamar to bring the food to him in the bedroom. She willingly obliges and takes the cakes to him. At this stage, she innocently figures that maybe he has become overly tired from sitting up and watching her cook, and now he needs to lie down and rest in bed while he eats. The situation degenerates from this point on. He takes hold of Tamar's hand and asks her to come and lie down with him.

Tamar is filled with shock and horror as she realises the tricky situation she now finds herself in. A hundred thoughts are racing through her mind as she frantically tries to decide how to handle this and what exactly she should do. She is consumed with disbelief that this is actually happening to her, and this feeling is mingled with fear and dread over the pending decision she faces.

She has several options. She could scream loudly, raising the alarm, but then she would have to explain to everyone what is going on. This would involve telling everyone the shameful facts, causing great embarrassment to both of them. This was a risky option, as she would still be tainted by the event. There was always the chance that Ammon might even deny it to save himself. This would force her to answer awkward questions, thus filling her with an overwhelming sense of shame. Even riskier is the other option – she must

Just Want to be Loved for Me...

somehow reason with Ammon logically and rationally to make him see how wrong all this was.

Tamar decides to at least try to talk her way out of it. This is often a good choice, and many women have been able to negotiate their way out of difficult situations and bring about changes using their wily communication skills in such a way that their attacker is left befuddled and thrown off track from what he intended to do to her.

She gives a convincing argument using four very clear reasons why he should not rape her. The first appeals to his knowledge and respect of the law. She tells him that what he is asking of her is a disgraceful thing. She refers to the law stated in Leviticus 18:11, which specifically forbids a brother from sleeping with his sister.

Secondly, Tamar describes to him the shame that will mark her, not him, and she reminds him that no good can come of this, and that she will be scorned forever after being defiled as a woman.

Her third argument rests on the fact that if he were to do such a thing, he would be like one of the fools in Israel. She further reminds him that by doing this to her, it could actually affect his right to inherit his father's throne. This tactic is designed to get Ammon to think of the long term effects for himself. She knows how much he wants to inherit the throne. By using this argument, she is forcing him to weigh a moment of temporary pleasure against his future inheritance.

Lastly, feeling distressed because she can sense that the other three reasons have not worked, she asks him to at least marry her first to legalise the situation. She tries really hard to persuade him that their father, King David, will not withhold her from him (Ammon) if only he will do things properly and just ask if he can marry her before taking her sexually.

Rape most foul

As you may have already guessed, he refuses to listen to anything she has to say. As far as he is concerned, he is now committed to the plan and will not be detracted from his aims. He is being short sighted and is driven by his physical needs. At this stage, he has lost the ability to think beyond the present moment and consider his future. He refuses even for a moment to see the big picture.

Ammon is driven by his intense passion for her, which sends him beyond the realm of reason. All of the feelings, anxieties and stresses of the last few months have culminated in a raging torrent of emotion that leaves him out of control, and now he is acting on his own animalistic instincts alone. He rapes her. Tamar is powerless to stop him. Her own physical strength is clearly no match for his. For her, time stands still as a hundred different thoughts crowd her mind in a swirl of confusion, each one demanding to be heard and dealt with. This was certainly not the way she had anticipated losing her virginity. She had imagined so many times what that would be like on her wedding night. She had envisioned her wedding dress, the ceremony, and even her husband so many times. It was an event she had looked forward to her whole life. She had also been brought up to revere and respect her body, and she had always looked forward to the day she would be able to offer it as the ultimate prize to her husband.

Just Want to be Loved for Me...

Ammon is forcing her down on the bed and is clumsily fumbling with her clothes. She panics and fights against him with all her might but to no avail. Her intermittent screams and pleas for him to stop are lost in the intensity of the moment. The more she fights him, the rougher and more excited he seems to become, and this terrifies Tamar beyond imagination.

Her cries are eventually silenced by the sharp searing pain that ravages her body and causes her to tremble and shake uncontrollably as Ammon enters her roughly. She holds her breath, hardly daring to breathe as she struggles to contain the pain that hits her body in wave upon wave of assault. Unbidden, she whimpers in pain and anguish as he thrusts in and out of her bruised body. He has no regard for her sense of decency, the agony he is forcing her to endure, or the fact that this is her first time. Ammon is only concerned about what he wants from her, which he considers to be his for the taking.

After what seems like an eternity, it is finally over, and Ammon releases his grip on Tamar and rolls over, spent. After a few minutes of awkward silence, he gets up from the bed and leaves her lying there. She turns onto her side and curls up in a ball, instinctively trying to protect herself. She wishes she was invisible, and if wishes were enough, she would have wished herself far away from the whole scene.

She feebly tries to cover her body and thus her shame as silent tears begin coursing down her beautiful cheeks and dripping onto the pillow below. She hurts all over and is embarrassed to find that her lower body is covered in a residue of both blood and wetness. There are no words to describe how she is feeling. She can hear Ammon moving around in the room, adjusting his clothes. The air is thick with a current of tension so potent that it is frightening. Tamar is afraid now and remains silent. She decides to wait until Ammon speaks.

Ammon finds that as soon as he has raped her, his feelings are completely reversed. He becomes consumed with such an intense hatred for Tamar that he promptly rejects her and tells her to go away. This no doubt has to do with his ability to now view the situation logically and begin to be consumed by the guilt of his wrongdoing.

The aftermath

Tamar is in a bad situation. She implores him to reconsider his rejection of her, telling him that this is even worse than the rape itself. She reminds him that there is still time for him to make this situation right before anyone knows the full extent of what has happened.

By this time, the evil intentions in Ammon's heart are so entrenched that he is not in a place to hear or think reasonably. His heart has become completely hardened to what he has done and there is not one ounce of decency or compassion left in him. As Tamar stands by struggling helplessly to make herself decent again, trying to convince him to do right by her, he calls his servant into the room. Ammon instructs him to put Tamar outside immediately and to bolt the door firmly behind her.

Tamar feels utterly abandoned. This ordeal has been more than she can bear, and there seems to be no way out of her situation and the consequences she will inevitably

Just Want to be Loved for Me...

face as an unmarried woman. As the virgin daughter of a king, Tamar would have traditionally been wearing a coat of many colours to show her position. Now, everything is about to change for her and she has no idea how to deal with it all. As a symbolic sign of her distress, she puts ashes on her head, tears her coat to pieces and with her hands on either side of her head she cries bitterly for all that has happened to her.

At a time in history when virginity was a crucial commodity of virtue and honour, she is totally distraught and feels that she has nothing to live for. All her childhood hopes and dreams of what her life would be like in the future lay shattered and in shreds, without the possibility for redemption at this stage. The future now stretches ahead like a curse in front of her. She almost certainly will never be married or have children now that she has been 'ruined'. She will have to settle for being the ever so nice, single Auntie Tamar who has no family of her own. From now on, men may still desire her, but it will be with the passion of lustful intentions, seeing her only as a distraction from their boring lives or marriages, but never seeing her as a potential bride or wife.

Tamar is rejected

Tamar is desperate to seek refuge somewhere safe. She ends up going to her brother Absalom's house. When he sees her crying so bitterly and hears her describe what has happened, he encourages her not to take it to heart, especially considering that Ammon is her brother. This has the effect of minimizing what has happened to her, and if that weren't bad enough, he follows this on by not taking a public stand against Ammon for what he has done to her.

The Bible tells us that Tamar remained 'desolate in his house'. This confirms that she never actually manages to get married or to have children. Added to this she now lives in a household where her other brother has brushed the event aside and told her not to take it to heart. This must have been utterly devastating for her. She is given no validation or support for what she has endured or for the dire consequences that will surely follow.

The Bible tells us that King David was also very angry about what happened but does not seem to have taken any concrete steps to punish Ammon for what he did. Absalom never speaks to or confronts Ammon about the incident, and on the face of it, everything seems forgotten. It looks as though Ammon has committed an unbelievable act of cruelty and has been able to get away with it altogether.

This was a triple blow for Tamar, one that threw her world upside down even further. She must have experienced deep-seated feelings of being isolated, cut off, and rejected, and as she replayed the events of that horrific night in her mind, she must have felt violated all over again. The three closest men in her life had each managed to let her down and had rejected her in her hour of need, a rejection that was particularly painful because she had been violated by a member of her own family. This added another level of shame and degradation to her already bruised ego and spirit. She knew without a doubt that had her attacker been a stranger, there would have been disastrous consequences for him. Her father and her two brothers would have rallied to her side and would have given their very lives in defending her honour.

Just Want to be Loved for Me...

However, there is a concerted attempt to hush things up and to keep the shame from being made public. This has the effect of exonerating Ammon while it pushes Tamar further into a world of isolation and shame brought on by the whole messy affair. There is an undercurrent of assumption that suggests that she must have done *something* to bring this upon herself. She is now the dirty little secret that must be kept by the whole family. **She** is the skeleton in the cupboard that no one must find out about.

This seems to be the same way in which an occurrence of incest is handled in modern times. Adults whose primary role is to love and protect their child(ren) molest and abuse them instead; somehow, these adults are sheltered and protected by the whole family, because keeping the family 'honour' by hiding such a secret takes precedence over taking care of the wounded child.

There is often very little regard for the child, who may have fought against all odds to speak out after being intimidated by the adult molester to keep the abuse a secret. Their worst fears are realised when adults do not believe them or they seriously question the accuracy of the child's account.

When all hell breaks loose and families are thrown into disarray, the child suffers all over again by feeling that it's his or her fault, since all of this is happening because of them. Those who do speak out are often berated for lying or causing shame and are driven into a situation where their ability to trust or to form healthy relationships is severely affected. Those who do not speak out are left isolated in their own world where they have no way to vent or to work through the issues. This will seriously impact any future relationships they may have too.

Tamar is in this very position. Her feelings of being at fault coupled with being let down by all three men in her family eventually grows into resentment, anger and shame. She must have also suffered emotions connected with the irreplaceable loss of her once-bright future, and because of this, she now has to find a suitable way to move on. Tamar has been forced to live out a life sentence when she was only just beginning to live life to the full. This stark reality is very different from anything she ever imagined when she daydreamed about her life as a woman. She will now have to come to terms with the unfairness of it all and figure out how she can cope, and none of that will be easy to do.

Absalom's revenge

We find out later on in the story that Absalom has not forgotten about the incident at all and has been nursing a secret hatred against Ammon for forcing himself on their sister. We are also told in the Bible that there is great resentment between the two brothers, which stems from the fact that they are both rivals for David's throne.

Absalom makes up his mind that these issues have to be dealt with and Ammon must pay for his actions. He begins to hatch a plan to get revenge. He is in no particular hurry, and we are reminded of the old adage that says that revenge is a dish best served cold. Absalom ends up having to wait until the timing is right and the opportunity presents itself. As it turns out, it takes him about two years to get his revenge.

Just Want to be Loved for Me...

As I read the story of Absalom's revenge, I was saddened by the amount of time and energy he must have expended over that two-year period. Imagine the wasted hours spent in negative contemplations, planning and plotting, the hatred fuelled and fed by the countless scenarios he must have played over and over in his mind. In each scenario he would have pictured the demise of Ammon in a different way, but each would have ended exactly the same – with Ammon losing and Absalom becoming the overall victor in the situation.

I am reminded that the Bible tells us that God says 'vengeance is mine....' We are therefore wasting our time plotting and scheming in order to get back at people. Sometimes we have the tendency to hold our enemies as prisoners in our own mental prison. This keeps the whole thing alive in our mind.

This mental imprisonment often involves intense feelings of hatred, dislike and resentment toward the one who has wronged us. Then, when we do eventually see these people in the course of our daily lives, we experience even more hurt and pain when we realise that they have moved on with their lives and we're still stuck in the mental prison we thought we had built for them. They have probably forgotten all about it and are not at all affected by the anger we still harbour for them. Meanwhile, we are still stuck in the past, with the person firmly locked behind bars in our mind. The issue has still not been dealt with, and the worst part of it is that in the time that has passed, we still have not been able to work through our anger, offer them forgiveness and then move on.

Bev Thomas-Graham

If this describes struggles that you are facing, please know that the only way to effectively deal with these kinds of difficulties is to release the situation to God in prayer. This finally releases the person from your mental prison. It also allows you to work through the issue and then move on. This allows God to work on your behalf and deal with the person for the wrong they have committed against you. I have often heard it said that when God deals with the other person, it is often far more sophisticated and effective than anything we could ever achieve using our limited strength and abilities.

We know from the Bible account that Absalom has not placed vengeance in the hands of God; instead, he has waited patiently for the time to be right to settle things as he sees fit. At last, the time finally comes for Absalom to get Ammon on his own so that he can at last begin to exact his revenge on him. He uses his cunning ways to persuade his father, King David, to allow Ammon to accompany him to Baal Hazor where he has sheepshearers waiting. He does this in a sneaky way, first insisting that David himself should come, and when David refuses (which Absalom knew he would do), Absalom then insists that David should at least let Ammon and the other brothers come.

The plot backfires

So, Absalom begins to execute the plot. He prepares a banquet fit for a king for all of them to enjoy. He tells his servants to watch out for when Ammon becomes very drunk on wine. When that happens, he tells the servants, they should watch for his signal, and when he gives the order, they should not be afraid to kill Ammon. Absalom knows that the servants are afraid of doing this, because if they kill

Just Want to be Loved for Me...

the king's son, they could lose their own lives too. He urges them not to worry, as he will take absolute responsibility for their actions. The servants are caught in a serious dilemma now. They are too afraid to kill Ammon, but they are also afraid to disobey a direct order from Absalom. In the end, they obey Absalom, and when they are given the order, they attack and kill Ammon in his drunken and intoxicated state.

The events take a turn for the worse and terror and pandemonium take over as everyone begins to panic. The people flee in all directions, anxious to escape in one piece. As soon as the other brothers realise what has happened, they quickly mount their mules and flee the scene as well. They head home urgently and are now seriously afraid for their own lives too. They are also traumatised to see their brother betrayed and struck down so coldly. At this stage, they have not understood that the plot was never about them and that they were never in any real danger.

Sadly, before they are even able to reach home, a messenger gets there first. He greets David with the news that Absalom has killed all David's sons in Baal Hazor and that not even one has survived. As a customary sign of grief, David tears his clothes and falls to the ground. He is completely numb with the pain of losing all of his sons at once. He feels bewildered and confused as to how this could have happened.

You can imagine the relief he feels when he learns that not all of his sons are dead, yet he is filled with grief that Ammon, his first-born son, has been killed. Absalom flees the area and stays away for three years. In effect, this means that David has lost him too. This proves to be a very difficult time for David.

Father and son are eventually reconciled, but this also ends badly when Absalom rebels against his father, causing him more stress and anxiety. Eventually, he is killed before ever making it to the throne as the king. This in effect renders all of his efforts in vain. All of the time spent in planning, scheming, anger and dishonesty have been wasted. We are often told that we reap what we sow. In Absalom's case, all of his negative attitudes, emotions and behaviour lead him to reach a very sad and unfulfilled end.

When negative life-changing events take place, there are seldom any winners. The impact of the event has a ripple effect, and the ripples reach far and wide and touch many different lives whether they are innocent or not.

Conclusion

One of the most pertinent things to note in this story is the breach of trust between Ammon and Tamar. Although this story centres on the issue of date rape, we must not forget that the relationship between them was one of being close family members. In times past as well as in modern times, women have faced abuse in the home from members of their own family. This is serious for many reasons. For most people, the home is a place of safety where they can escape to when the pressures of life become too much to bear. It acts as a sanctuary of protection against the outside world. The home is a place where we are loved and protected, and we can relax and just be ourselves. This gets completely turned on its head when the home itself becomes the battlefield and where people need to find a sanctuary outside of it. Imagine

Just Want to be Loved for Me...

being afraid to come home after school or work or being afraid of someone in your household.

Millions of people live their lives with this kind of fear and oppression inflicted on them by the very people who should protect them. It is an unspeakable horror when trusted family members end up being the perpetrators of abuse, both physical and mental, within the home environment. Too often, their victims' inward cries of hurt, pain and humiliation go unheard along with their desperate pleas for help.

We never do find out what happened to Tamar after Ammon was killed. We will never know what kind of life she ended up with eventually. Her story, as recorded in the Bible, sadly ends here. However, we do know that the suffering she experienced would have caused a ripple effect that touched many, many lives, with each ripple bringing its own level of disappointment, broken dreams and pain. We realise that things do not happen in isolation but instead always end up having an effect on others.

I believe that whatever happened to Tamar, she must have only been able to face each day with renewed strength and vigour because of her trust and reliance on her creator. Only God would have been able to reach down into the depths of her spirit to bring calm to her frazzled mind and peace to her life. Only he would have been able to pour his anointing all over her, to salve the pain and to bring her to a place of healing.

It is often very difficult for people to fully understand what Tamar must have gone through (unless they've experienced incest themselves). She probably continued to live her life in a way that reflected who she really was originally. People meeting her later in life and feeling the warmth and love emanating from her spirit would never know the secret pain and heartaches she had endured. Consider the people who surround you in your life right now; you would be surprised to find what lies beneath their cheerful exterior.

I remember an old song by Smokey Robinson of Motown fame called "The Tears of a Clown." The song is about a clown whose job is to be the life and soul of the party and to make everyone laugh. In the quiet, still times, the clown is allowed to be who he really is, and he is finally able to shed the tears of loneliness, heartache and pain he carries with him all the time. The clown outfit allows him to hide behind a mask so that the rest of the world can never see the pain that lies behind it. This keeps his human vulnerability hidden. God is the only one who can see behind this mask, and he is never fooled by outward appearances of happiness.

Some people seem so cheerful all the time, but actually, they are hiding behind the very real pain they feel all the time. Others appear so miserable and outwardly seem to hate the world. The pain and disappointment they feel has become so intense that they are no longer able to cope by maintaining a deceptive mask. They often feel bitter and unable to hope that they will ever be able to trust anyone again.

As Christians, it is important for us not to judge these people, as we do not know what they have been through. We cannot proudly state that we would be any different, because if we had faced what they have had to endure, we might find it even harder to cope. That person may be on the verge of

Just Want to be Loved for Me...

giving up, or worse yet, they may wish that they could end their life. A kind word spoken to a person in this situation can make all the difference, even if they have treated you harshly. Even if we cannot physically make things better for them, we can include them in our prayers and ask God to act in their lives. If you know someone who is carrying a heavy load of pain, anger and frustration, pray for God to give them strength through the difficulties they face, and ask him to comfort and keep them in his will as they make their way through this trial.

This is what would have been at the base of Tamar's strength during her time of suffering. Her family were all strong people of God, and they would have interceded for her in prayer when all seemed lost. In addition, they would have physically been her strength, her support and her comfort through both the high and the low points.

You may be surprised to find out that there are many Tamars around you, taking each day as it comes, living in survival mode and not able to see or plan ahead; wanting so badly for things to be different and never really sure how they can make the changes that are needed to put their lives back on track. Oftentimes they feel isolated and trapped in their situation, unable to share their feelings with anyone. It could be that you are a kind of Tamar and may be struggling to find your way out of a bad situation.

Be encouraged that God has the answer, and all you need to do is to ask for his help, trust in his word and allow him to work in your life. Only then will you come to a place where you can move on and change your life.

Chapter Four

The 'Matey' Syndrome

Hannah's Story

Introduction

The word 'matey' is used predominantly in the Caribbean and especially in Jamaica. It is also the word for one of the many spices used to make a delicious curry dish. The word itself is used to describe the relationship that exists between two women who share the sexual favours of the same man. One will inevitably be the wife or the official partner, and the other will be the 'spicy' element – the woman on the side.

This situation can be the bane of the modern woman's life, and it is growing more common. Over the years, I have spoken to a wide variety of women from many different cultures and age groups. This problem appears to be widespread. Many of the women I have ministered to have experienced it themselves. Lots of others know at least one other woman who has been through it.

This topic can therefore be a very emotional one. People who experience it find themselves struggling with a plethora of emotions that are often conflicting and not very rational. These emotions range from jealousy, anger and betrayal, to feelings of being let down, loss of confidence and loss of the ability to trust. The only good thing about the 'matey' situation is that everyone seems to have a view about it; therefore, it is a subject that can really get people going.

It is not surprising to realise that the Bible deals with this issue. There are several women mentioned in the Bible whose difficulties arose predominantly from having to deal with another female who was in a personal relationship with the woman's husband or partner. I am in good company with Solomon, the writer of the book of Ecclesiastes, when

I say that there is nothing new under the sun. We spend a lot of time trying to say how different things are now or how much worse things are in modern society compared to the 'good old days'. Yet the truth is that there is nothing new; everything has already been thought of, tried or done by someone, somewhere at some time or another.

Background

In this section, we will examine the story of a young woman, and we will learn how she coped with this very difficult situation. Her name is Hannah, and her full story is told in chapter 1 of the book of First Samuel in the Old Testament.

The story is set in the backdrop of the historical account of the chosen people of God. The people are in a difficult situation, and they are crying out desperately to God, needing Him to hear and respond to them. This is the period in Israelite history before the kings emerge, and when the people are being led by judges.

This is a very special time, and God is about to do something awesome for his people. He wants to respond to their continuous prayers for help because he was getting ready to release the last of the judges into the world. This man would be the greatest of all the judges and would come to be viewed as the first great prophet to emerge after the time of Moses. This judge would lead Israel until the time came for him to hand over the mantle of leadership to the new era when the kings would rule.

Just Want to be Loved for Me...

Hannah's story begins

Hannah was one of the two wives of Elkanah, who was a Levite. The story opens with an account of their yearly trip to the Tabernacle at Shiloh to worship and to offer sacrifices. Hannah's 'matey' was a woman called Penninah, and the two did not get on very well. At the bottom of this conflict was the fact that Penninah resented Hannah as an adversary for her husband's affections. In her own eyes, ***she*** was the perfect wife. She was the one who had cared for her husband, and even more importantly, she had given him a number of children, including sons. She regarded Hannah as a waste of space because she had proved to be barren. Hannah had never been able to add to Elkanah's household. She had therefore never managed to fulfil her role as a wife and mother.

The women on both sides of this scenario seem to suffer from many mixed emotions. On the face of it, they both appear to have accepted their fate in cultural terms. This means that they had belonged to their father before marriage, and now they belong to their husband. Their marriages would have been arranged by their parents, and even as women, they would have very little say or opinion in the matter. However, it was still only natural and human that they would feel jealously, as they were rivals. They would both continuously strive to attain the upper hand in their husband's affections.

This arrangement seems to go against the original intentions of God when he created humankind. The special intimacy and bond created by marriage is second to none, and this intimacy is intended to be savoured and enjoyed by two people of opposite sexes.

I spell this out because today we are surrounded by a variety of relationships, and in the modern atmosphere of political correctness, we feel almost forced to accept these living arrangements as normal, irrespective of our own personal (and spiritual) stance on them. People who do not conform are viewed as ignorant and intolerant. In some cases, people who are also employees may even find themselves in breach of the local laws if they expressly declare their views on the matter. This may result in stiff legal penalties or disciplinary action at their workplace. In serious cases, this may even lead to dismissal and affect the ability of the person to secure further work.

The special intimacy between two people who are married in the eyes of the law and the Lord enables them to be joined as one. It forces all the barriers to come tumbling down. Both people surrender and become lost in the will and desire of the other. Gone is the mask that people hide behind in the normal course of life. There is openness, trust and love between them in the intimacy of marriage. This special bond creates exclusivity between them.

The bond of marriage is so special that it is difficult to believe that this intimacy could ever be replicated with anyone else in a simultaneous relationship. Women in particular give and share their whole being with a man during lovemaking. It causes them to become consumed with conflicting emo tions in a crisis. This is what happens when they realise that their partner is sharing the same feelings, emotions and intimacy with someone else.

This is what both Hannah and Penninah would have regularly experienced being married to the same man. It is

Just Want to be Loved for Me...

also what haunts the modern woman when she finds out about a 'matey' she is in competition with for her husband's affections. This is especially hard for the wife if she is under the assumption that she is the only woman in his life at the time (which is natural for her to think, but that assumption is really a misapprehension).

The fact that Hannah had not been able to have children created a decided imbalance in the relationship between the two women. It firmly put Penninah in a more powerful position. In the true spirit of the 'matey', she wasted no time or opportunity to tease and belittle Hannah. She made sure to flaunt every new pregnancy, and at every opportunity, Penninah would have made a fuss in front of Hannah over her cute and cuddly babies and her perfect family. She would have reminded Hannah over and over again about Hannah's barrenness, which in essence was her failure as a woman. Penninah made sure that Hannah stayed firmly in her inferior place in the home. She would have reinforced this continually to ensure that Hannah knew how much better Penninah was as a wife who had pleased her husband.

The 'Matey'

In the modern day, especially in western societies, it is often the case that women go for a long time in the mistaken belief that they are in a monogamous relationship. When they find out about the 'matey', it throws their safe little world into a chasm of pain, confusion and bewilderment. Most of this negative energy is directed toward the 'matey', not toward the cheating husband.

I have often wondered why a woman would hate, curse and seek to harm the 'matey' instead of directing her anger toward the man who has cheated on her. He is the one who shares an obligation to maintain a monogamous relationship with the woman he is committed to (hopefully his wife). The 'matey' probably does not even know about the wife. The cheating husband probably has the 'matey' convinced that he is single and available and that the 'matey' is the 'only one' for him. If she is also single and available, she may have the impression that she is in a faithful and monogamous relationship with this man.

Sometimes, women become career mistresses. You often find that they too have been hardened by the whole sorry process. They often have no loyalties, and usually they have been victims of the 'matey syndrome' at some stage in their life. A career mistress will not invest too much of herself in any casual relationship. She will make herself perfectly content to have as much of the man as he is able to give her. The mistress will have programmed herself to no longer crave a soul mate with whom she can totally join herself heart and soul. There is the innate feeling that it is impossible to find such a person. She will be totally disillusioned and regard the whole thing as some kind of fairly tale or fantasy. Women who fall into the pattern of being career mistresses are often seeking a kind of dream existence, an idealistic world where they can escape from their dreary lives.

I have spent many years working with women. In doing so, I have come to realise that a woman is often in a state of shock when she discovers a 'matey' in her relationship. Her emotions go into complete overdrive, and her thoughts become a mass of confusion as she tries to make sense of it all. This makes her unable to think logically or to process the information reasonably. She is incapable of accepting that the man she has shared such intimacy with could commit such a cold act of deception. She is convinced she *knows* this man intimately; they have shared so many private and special moments together. She knows his secrets and his passions, and it is difficult for her to comprehend that another woman shares this intimacy with him as well.

We often tend to judge people by what we would or would not do if we were in their situation, and most women feel incapable of committing such an act of betrayal. Therefore, it is hard to imagine that a man they care about so deeply is able to betray them so willingly and easily.

This leads many women to think, *the poor man couldn't help himself! In his weakness, he was simply unable to resist temptation*. Based on all that a woman in this situation knows about her man, she is convinced there is no way he could cheat on her of his own choice. It must be that the 'matey', temptress that she is, has somehow beguiled him. She must have wantonly pursued him and somehow forced him. It is so easy for women who've been cheated on to blame a mysterious woman they do not know for luring their man away, because it keeps them from having to face the awful truth that their man has chosen to be unfaithful to them. It is much easier to blame the 'matey' with all the negativity, the evil intentions and the action-packed, conniving plan to get another woman's man by any means possible.

I thank God that this thinking on the part of a wronged woman is usually only temporary and eventually passes. The woman is then finally able to think through the situation logically and consciously, not reacting on unconscious fears and gut feelings. She then comes to a logical realisation of exactly what has taken place. It is only then that she is able to put the responsibility for the betrayal squarely on the shoulders of the *real* guilty person – the man!

It takes varying lengths of time for women to process through to this moment of realisation. In the case of some women, this may never happen, and they settle into victim mode, accepting this as their inevitable lot in life. When that happens, the woman is never able to move beyond it. She becomes bitter, and all her future choices are affected by her bitterness. She may feel that she can never allow herself to go through that painful process again and will choose to remain alone rather than risk the vulnerability that comes with loving a man.

If she is able to move on into a new relationship, it may be blighted by her past negative experiences. The new man in her life will have a long way to go in proving that he is actually different from all the men in the past who have hurt her. He will be constantly judged and mistrusted, and this will definitely affect how intimately close they can be. Depending on how bad it becomes, the new man may even find it difficult to stick around. This will only serve to confirm the woman's negative views of men.

The third result may be that the woman decides to take charge of the situation herself. She learns to control her emotions almost to the point of suppressing them, and she consciously reduces the amount of time and effort she puts into any new relationship. On the face of it, this seems like the ideal scenario. However, any control she has may be short lived. After a while, she will begin to feel unfulfilled and still crave the level of intimacy she knows is possible but that somehow seems elusive because of the walls she has built around herself.

Just Want to be Loved for Me...

A woman's lot

Are any of these scenarios any more painful than actually being in Hannah's position? Imagine what it would be like to know all about your rival and have to live in the same household with her. First of all, Hannah has to deal with the fact that she has no power or authority over her life or future. She is not in a position where she can demand Elkanah to commit to her alone. She cannot force him to stay in a monogamous relationship with her. This is something that many women in Biblical times struggled with.

Hannah was very unhappy indeed. She was completely fed up and dismayed with feeling like a lesser person. Each year at the Tabernacle certain offerings, prayers and sacrifices would be made, then portions of the celebration meal would be divided up amongst the families.

In their household, Penninah always got more than Hannah did because she had given Elkanah children, which ranked her higher than Hannah. Elkanah, however, loved both his wives and knew of the rivalry between them. He especially loved Hannah and would always give her a slightly larger portion than a barren wife would normally get.

This time, he notices that she is not eating and appears upset. Her eyes are red from crying, and her face is pale and bereft of any emotion. He hates to see her upset. He instantly knows what has happened, and he becomes annoyed and cross that this issue has risen up between the women yet again. He cannot even bear to hear the details of what has happened again *this* time! Despite the fact that his two wives often hid their quarrels from him, he knew enough from looking at her to understand that this latest spat had affected

Hannah deeply. He could only imagine the hateful things that may have been said to her and prayed that it had not come to physical blows again.

Elkanah is frustrated with this situation. He has done everything he can to show Hannah how much he loves her and that she indeed holds a very special place in his heart. Yet nothing seems to change her feelings of inadequacy, and so she remains distraught.

During certain periods, he becomes very distressed by this situation as well. It was a common practice at that time for men to have more than one wife. It seemed to Elkanah that this set-up worked fairly well, at least among his friends and acquaintances, but he could not seem to bring peace between his two wives.

In trying to manage the situation he would often become so distressed that he would challenge both Hannah and Penninah and question their love for him. Knowing how much Hannah wanted a son, Elkanah once actually asked her if he was not worth more than ten sons to her. Hannah truly loved her husband and would do anything to please him, but it was plain to her, just by the very fact that he would ask such a question, that he just did not understand her. There was a level of pain, frustration and emptiness to being childless that Elkanah would never be able to fully understand as a man.

It was the pain of being barren – of not being able to fulfil the most elemental part of a woman's role. This basic need left unfulfilled impacted Hannah's physical, emotional and spiritual well being.

Just Want to be Loved for Me...

Being unable to bear a child, Hannah must have spent time pondering what was wrong with her and trying to find the meaning of her life and her purpose in the world. For one thing, if Elkanah died there would be no one to take care of her. She would be left alone to depend on the charity of others, possibly even from Penninah and her children. This would feel like a fate worse than death. In a society where your status as a woman depended on your ability to be a good wife and mother, Hannah would have failed miserably if she never produced any children. She would always feel not quite as good as the other women. There would always be an empty longing that would eat away at her self-respect and confidence for the rest of her life.

It was definitely not a good place to be. Furthermore, it was hard for Elkanah to fully appreciate the depth and severity of Hannah's situation, thus making her lonely inner struggles even worse. The sad thing is that Elkanah probably never completely understood what Hannah was going through.

The story of Hannah is one of courage and immeasurable faith. She is extraordinary because she was not one to accept the fate that would surely emerge from her current situation. Given her limited bargaining power in society as a woman, she chose to take the issue to the highest authority she knew. She was not going to sit around and feel sorry for herself anymore. She is going to fight to achieve her childhood dreams of the life she expected to have one day as a married woman.

Hannah was also smart enough to know that no human could change her situation. She would have been aware that even though her husband loved and adored her, he was unable to make things better because her barrenness (or fertility, for that matter) was in God's hands. Even his attempts to stop Penninah and her cruel taunts had not amounted to much. It seems that he believed in choosing the path of least resistance and only wanted a quiet, simple life. He did not want to be a referee for his two wives with their constant bickering. In many ways, he secretly hoped that if he ignored the situation it would eventually sort itself out. Even though their squabbles clearly affected him, he never fully engaged with them on the matter. He also never took sole responsibility as the head of the household to resolve the issue.

Penninah

In many ways, it seems as though there are only victims in this story. All three members of this love triangle are locked away in their own pain and discomfort, struggling to cope and longing to find a way out.

From the Biblical account of this story, it seems that Penninah herself is not an evil, vindictive person. It also logically follows that she too has issues relating to the insecurities of being in this lover's triangle of a marriage. Even though she has the upper hand as the wife who has borne children, she secretly knows that Elkanah has a much greater love for Hannah, and this knowledge eats away at Penninah.

The worst part is that despite all her efforts to please her husband in every way she can, she still has not managed to secure his undivided attention and love. She feels much resentment over this and just cannot understand why he would want to waste emotions and time on Hannah, who

Just Want to be Loved for Me...

has not even been able to fulfil her basic role as a woman and as a wife.

Penninah longs to be loved and desired exclusively by her husband. She longs to be his only girl, his 'little wifey' and the apple of his eye. This is the way that God originally intended it to be when he created the first man and woman and placed them in the Garden of Eden. The minute we humans begin to change things round and operate outside of God's divine purpose, problems begin to emerge. In this case, the very act of having more than one wife is unnatural and is bound to create difficulties. When God created man, it was his intention that the man should work in line with the purpose for which he was created. This was supposed to be with the aid of a helper, a wife to co-exist with him and work beside him. The roles become confused when a man tries to do this with more than one wife.

Both Hannah and Penninah are aware of what their culture says about sharing husbands, and they accept it as a matter of course. They both know that they do not have the power to change things. There is no official 'girl power'. Yet although they accept this situation as normal, they clearly do not like it, and it does not feel natural to them to share a husband in this way.

Hannah has enough

On this occasion, Hannah decides that enough is enough. She takes herself away from the others, and as she contemplates her situation, her eyes well up again with fresh tears of anger and frustration. As they begin to fall, her heart inwardly grieves for her situation. I believe that Hannah had already been practising the **PUSH** principle, which is to **P**RAY **U**NTIL **S**OMETHING **H**APPENS. Right now, she is despondent because there appears to be no change in her situation, but Hannah is strong and is not one to give up without a fight. This time, in desperation, she takes it a step further.

This time is different; the situation has placed her in a position where there seems to be no way out. Her face becomes awash with the salty tears of pain, humiliation and distress. She opens up her heart and tentatively begins a conversation with God. As she begins to communicate, she is overcome with emotion. Hannah then pours out all that is in her heart. She is so bitter about everything by now and is driven by great emotion. This is a different kind of prayer and is often called a prayer with groaning. This is where the prayer comes from the depths of your spirit and encompasses intense emotional distress or need. Hannah cries out to God, begging him to change her circumstances, pleading with him to bless her with a son. So great is her desperation and need that she promises God that if he grants her this child, she will dedicate him to the Lord's service after he has been weaned.

Hannah's prayer is intense, as it comes from the depths of her inner being. She prays silently and fervently with only her lips moving. There is not a single sound coming from her. Unknown to her, she is being watched by Eli the priest. He is very concerned about how long she has stayed kneeling at the altar.

Eli finds himself being a bit judgmental. As he watches Hannah, he thinks, *Oh, here's another one. There have been too many instances lately of people coming into the Tabernacle and behaving inappropriately. How can there be such a lack*

Just Want to be Loved for Me...

of respect and reverence for God's holiest place? At this yearly event many people came to the Tabernacle as a matter of ritual, not out of devotion. Some even treated the occasion as a social event. Eli knew that this clearly went against the whole plan of God, who wanted the people to come with their hearts humbled, and for their prayers and offering to be in communion with him. Eli and the other priests were always on the lookout for people who were not there to be reverent.

After watching Hannah for some time, Eli is convinced that she is not behaving as she should be doing. He notices that she looks completely out of it, and even though she appears to be mumbling to herself, there is still not a sound coming from her lips. He approaches Hannah and angrily rebukes her for being drunk in the Tabernacle.

Having been deep in prayer, Hannah is now brought back to reality with a bump. She has been so intent on talking to God that she has not been aware of what anyone watching her would think. She has simply been giving her all to God. In casting aside her earthly cares, she has been completely unaware of anything or anyone else. This time of prayer has been about her and her relationship with God. She is embarrassed that Eli could even think she was being disrespectful in the Tabernacle. She immediately responds to him humbly apologising for her behaviour. When she explains her full situation to Eli, his heart is filled with compassion for her. He reassures her that the power of God is very real, and can change anything. Eli encourages Hannah to continue in her prayers and to never give up. He then joins her in prayer and prays a special blessing on her, too.

Prayer changes things

As so often happens after a deep prayer with God, Hannah feels a big weight lift off her body. This is probably also the moment when her previously stooped shoulders straighten up for the first time in a long while and her heart begins to feel light. It has been so long since she has felt this kind of relief. She smiles for the first time in a very long time, and her once sad face is now lit up and transformed, as beautiful as ever but now abundantly happy. Her eyes twinkle with a spark of hope and joy. There is a definite skip to her step as she leaves the Tabernacle to make her way home, this time with much eagerness to get there.

She feels at peace now in the full knowledge that God will take care of her situation once and for all. Whichever way he chooses to solve it, she knows that it will be the right decision for her. She knows that she must keep her trust and faith in him. After all, her life is totally in his hands. God alone will have to take care of her in her old age if she is not blessed with a child. If he did choose to answer her prayer, well that would be so awesome.

She happily rejoins the others and is able to join in and enjoy the celebration meal with them. This lifts the mood for the whole family. Elkanah notices that she seems different somehow and is actively taking part in the celebrations, something she has never really done before. He had noticed earlier when she had slipped away (to pray at the Tabernacle), and he had fought himself not to follow her. He could not bear another confrontation with her, and he didn't need three guesses to tell him what the matter was. Penninah had looked unconcerned when Hannah departed without explanation and was actually relieved that she could sit alone

Just Want to be Loved for Me...

with her husband and their children for once without that nuisance Hannah hanging about.

Elkanah was at a loss as to how to manage the tense situation between his two wives. The other men had advised him that he should leave these matters alone. He should let the women sort it out among themselves, they said. Elkanah did not have the answers, but he was still concerned about it. He had still anxiously looked out for Hannah after she had gone, being careful not to let Penninah see him watching and waiting as he willed Hannah to return so that he could see that she was alright.

Just as he is about to head out after Hannah because she has been gone far too long for his liking, she suddenly re-appears just in sight down the village lane making her way toward the house. He cannot help but notice how she walks with her head up, her face alight, her back straight, almost with a jaunty step of happiness.

Where has she been? Elkanah wonders. No matter – he will find out eventually. All that matters is that she seems so happy now. Whatever had happened to lift her mood, he is grateful for it. For the first time in a very long time, he was able to sit with his family and enjoy a good meal in a relaxed atmosphere.

God hears and answers

Shortly after this, Hannah's prayer is answered and she is delighted to discover that she is in fact pregnant. She has now personally experienced the wonder of God's character and of his mercy toward her in changing her fortune. She thanks him that Penninah's taunts have been silenced. She gives praise for the fact that her past feelings of emptiness, longing, misery and shame are all gone.

Hannah is filled with such joy that she cannot find the words to describe the way she feels. God has literally heard and answered her prayer. Her faith, love and commitment to God are at an all-time high.

The whole of First Samuel chapter 2 is dedicated to her song of praise. Singing invokes responses from your whole body, your mind and your soul. It is one of the highest forms of praise. There is another record in the Bible of this kind of praise found in the book of Luke chapter 1 verse 46 onwards. This is when Mary finds out that she is pregnant too. She also has a song of praise and exaltation to God for the miracle he has given her.

In fact, Hannah joins a long line of women who have experienced the pain and bitterness of being barren. These women include Sarah, the mother of Isaac, and Rebecca, the mother of Esau and Jacob in the Old Testament. There is also Elizabeth, the mother of John the Baptist in the New Testament. All these women experienced a miracle in their lives. Their sons were not only a blessing in answer to several years of prayer, but they also fulfilled crucial parts of God's plan for humankind.

Hannah's little miracle was a healthy baby boy. She named him Samuel, which means 'God hears', because she asked God for him and he heard her prayer. Hannah was overjoyed, but her joy was filled with bittersweet sadness. She has mixed emotions because she has been blessed with the one thing that she wanted the most – a son. Yet true to her promise to God, she knows that she will never be able

Just Want to be Loved for Me...

to raise Samuel herself. As soon as he is weaned she will have to bring him to Shiloh and let him live there at the Tabernacle. Elkanah is a Levite, and as such, Samuel will have to serve the priesthood when he becomes an adult anyway. According to Hannah's promise, he will serve from an earlier age and will actually grow up and be trained in the Tabernacle.

Samuel was a precious gift from God to Hannah. He was a gift that she would have marvelled at as she cradled him in her arms. She would have examined him from head to toe and taken in every detail of his perfect little being. She knew that she would have to delight in him as much as possible during the short time that she would have with him. Her heart swelled with love and pride as she gazed down at him. At last, she was fulfilled as a woman, a mother and a wife. She would be free from teasing and taunts about her infertility. The emotional pain she had endured would now cease.

Hannah may have had a shaky start in terms of motherhood. However, it took strong character for Hannah to give up the son she longed for and loved more than anyone or anything. God saw all of this and would reward her greatly later on. He knew she was a faithful person, as she had trusted him with the most difficult issues in her life.

True to her promise, Hannah takes little Samuel to the Tabernacle when the time comes, and she and Elkanah sacrifice a bull there. This was done as a symbolic way to show that Samuel's life would be dedicated to God. Eli, the priest, was pleased to welcome Samuel, and he promised to train him well. Hannah reminded him of the day when he had thought she had been drunken in the Tabernacle. She thanked Eli for the compassion he showed her when he realised her true story. They reminisced together as they remembered how they had prayed together afterwards. They also marvelled at God's awesome power and grace as they looked at Samuel.

Hannah looked over her precious son one last time with a proud motherly smile as she presented him to Eli and walked away, holding back her tears mixed with joy and sadness. Eli was filled with humility as he realised the important role he must now play in this special boy's life. He knew that God had a purpose for Samuel and a calling on his life. He felt honoured to be chosen as a vessel through which God's love and purpose would be manifested.

So it was that Hannah left Samuel at the Tabernacle and returned home. She visited her son regularly and brought new linen robes to fit him as he grew taller and bigger each year. As the story ends, we read that God blesses Hannah with many more sons and daughters. This is the reward for her continued commitment and faithfulness to God's will. At last, she is fulfilled and happy. Now she will never be alone and her future will never be uncertain again.

Samuel was a precious gift to Hannah at a time when she needed him most. He grew up to be the last and greatest of the judges and was on hand to bring in the reign of the kings. This was at a time when the people were discontented and no longer willing to accept God as their sovereign king. They demanded a physical earthly king. Samuel's role in anointing the first king, Saul, and especially in choosing young David to be the king after Saul (see 1 Samuel 16), was crucial in bringing this about. Samuel was also a faithful judge and was regarded as a great prophet.

Be encouraged by Hannah's life

Hannah was just a regular and simple woman who felt that life was passing her by. Tormented daily by her 'matey', she felt empty and unfulfilled. She had no idea that she would come to be used so greatly of God. She could never have known that her faithfulness and devotion to the Lord would be forever recorded in the Bible and that she would be remembered for all time. She was the mother of Samuel, who would grow up to play such a key role in the leadership and history of her people.

We never know how and when God may use us to fulfil his plan for the world. One thing is certain, though: We are all here for a purpose. It may be that your purpose is not for something as great as Hannah's was. Nonetheless, your purpose in the body of Christ matters just as in the physical body everything has a purpose. This is from the largest organs to the tiniest cell. Malfunction in any of them causes the body to not work properly, and this can lead to many health complications. The body totally depends on each member, cell, and organ to perform its purpose well and to contribute towards the well being of the whole.

This is the same for us. God has a distinctive purpose for each of us. This purpose in turn will be important to the working of his overall plan for humankind. Whether your contribution is large or small, it is still vitally important. The overall plan may therefore be adversely affected if you do not perform your part.

If you do not know what your purpose is, you need to talk to God about it urgently. If you have ever wondered about the meaning of life or if you have ever thought there must be more to life than this, let me assure you that there is. Only you can know your unique purpose, and the best place to start to discover it is with your Creator.

If you do not know God as your heavenly Father, then first you need to make that connection. In telling Hannah's story, I have striven to give you an insight into how the past is inevitably bound up in the present. Her story also reminds us once again that there is nothing new under the sun. God is the same today as he was yesterday and will be tomorrow. He alone can be your ever-present source of help. He actually wants you to have a closer relationship with him but you have to choose to follow him. It is not his way to force you even though he clearly could if he wanted to. His greatest joy is to see you choose, of your own free will, to love him and be close to him.

It is not hard to love the Lord and live for him every day. Having known him my whole life, I can honestly say that I cannot imagine what life would be like without him. For me the thought is scary and unthinkable. I am reminded of Psalm 139, where we read about how God made us. We were wonderfully made right down to the last detail, with such care and dedication. Nothing was left to chance. This is because you are too important to him and he desires the best for you. This is the reason that I could never be without him.

Even when I was not walking with God the way I should, I still had a relationship with him. I had already been blessed in knowing him as a child. It was the most precious gift that my parents ever gave to me. This meant that no matter how hard life became, I always knew that I could call out to him and that he would never let me down. God was someone stable and faithful to hold on to when I clearly was not worthy enough to even call his name. Deep down I knew that he loved me in spite of myself, even though I had rejected him to follow other worldly pursuits. I am grateful that through his love and mercy I was able to make my way back to him to fulfil my purpose before it was too late.

If you want to make a start, begin by talking to him and recognising who he is and what he has done for you. Ask him to forgive you for your past mistakes and sins and to come into your life. Let him know that you are now ready to commit yourself to him. That is really all it takes for you to take the first step. After that, all that is left for you to do is to get to know him better and to develop a relationship with him.

If you already know God as your Lord and Saviour, now is the time to take your relationship with him a step further. Let him help you to discover why you are here so that you can step into your destiny. This may be scary, because if you are like most people, you do not like change. We tend to be creatures of habit and do not take kindly to changes. However, you need to be ready to move out of your comfort zone to allow God to take you to the next level. Remember that God will not impose himself on you. He is waiting for your move; what are you waiting for?

Talk to him and let him know that you are willing to release your destiny into his will. You may be thinking, *I've prayed that before, Bev, and nothing happened*. If that's the case, make sure you mean it this time and be ready to allow him to lead the way. There is nothing to be afraid of. Just reach out your hand to him and he will grasp it in his.

Victory over your situation

It may be that you are a Hannah suffering at the hands of your 'matey'. God knows your pain and he hurts every time you hurt. He does not want you to be in this painful situation. It could be that you have tried to change your situation but find that you can't.

Deep down you know that your partner will never leave the other woman, and she quite enjoys having a relationship with no formal ties. You want to leave him and have even tried to do so, but somehow you feel that you cannot survive on your own. It may be that you have financial ties together or even children.

I have known many women who were taunted mercilessly by their 'matey'. I have heard them hurling abuse at the poor wife, saying things like 'you wash his clothes, iron them, feed him, and I get all the fun and none of the drudgery. I wouldn't swap places with you in a million years. Keep up the good work; he's looking good just now – for me!' Other taunts are directed towards a wife who has never managed to have children. 'You may be his wife but I am his baby's mother; you can't breed and give him the thing he wants the most!'

Sometimes the wife or partner finds herself subjected to hostile and dirty phone calls, stalking, hate mail and even physical abuse at the hands of her 'matey'. I have even come across the case of the 'matey' who deliberately leaves telltale signs of her presence in places where the wife or

Just Want to be Loved for Me...

partner will find it. This may be her lipstick, earring, or other personal items that will betray her presence in the man's life, something she does with great pride. Whilst this may appear accidental, it is often the case that these items are strategically placed in order to have maximum effect, especially on the unsuspecting wife. The 'matey' will get a sense of satisfaction in watching the man backtrack his way out of the situation when he is caught and trying to explain what he's been doing. The 'matey' will also gain strength in what she is doing if the wife or partner is foolish enough to accept her man's feeble excuses. The 'matey' convinces herself that if the wife or partner is stupid enough to believe *that* story, then she deserves to be cheated on.

If you are coping with a 'matey' in your relationship, the one thing you are probably definitely sure of is that you have never managed to solve this situation on your own. Worse still, no one around you seems to have the answer either. You feel helpless because you simply do not have what it takes to move on with your life. So the three of you co-exist miserably and the situation just drags on.

You feel like there is no point in talking about it anymore. You just want to be left alone to stew quietly in your misery. You feel that no one understands what you are going through and wouldn't be able to help you even if you did tell them.

Take courage from Hannah's strength of will and determination. One day she decided that enough was enough. She had nothing left to lose. She turned the situation over to God on that day in the temple. You can do the same.

Take heart; God is there. He understands you right to the very core of your being. Remember, he created you. He alone can help you turn this situation around. His strength and love can cover you and give you the peace of mind that you so badly crave. Only then will you be able to recognise your true worth and understand how precious you are in his sight. You will also begin to understand that you have a purpose that only *you* can fulfil. God will show you the way; you just need to give him a chance.

If you're the 'matey', there is hope for you too

If you are the 'matey', then you probably sense that you are one of the most hated people around, and the chances are that you could not care less. You have become jaded to the whole situation, and to things like true love, loyalty and commitment. As the saying goes, you have "been there, done that." You are definitely not in this relationship for the approval of others. On the face of it, you are hardened, and this is because of all that you have been through. You are there to take what you can get on your own terms.

A long time ago, you gave up the dream of having a one to one personal relationship. You are probably convinced that everyone is cheating and being unfaithful and so there is no point expecting the impossible. The 'dream' is exactly that and firmly belongs in the realms of fairy tales. These are the visions that every little girl dreams of before she painfully grows up to realise that the truth is nothing like that. You may be one of those women who live by the motto of not feeling sorry for any woman whose man you are in a 'matey' relationship with right now. After all, who felt sorry for you when another woman did the same with your man?

Just Want to be Loved for Me...

Did they care about how it might affect you or destroy your life and family? It's life, and that's all there is to it.

Earlier I spoke about Penninah, the woman who was Hannah's 'matey'. She was not an evil person or a hardcore slut, but she was responding to her own insecurities about what life had dealt her. If you are like Penninah, please know that it really does not have to be this way. I write these things because I care for you. There is a way for you to deal with your own issues and move on. This will take away the hurt that you have kept shut away deep in your soul for so long. It will also restore your faith in relationships. Only then can the softer and more caring side of your nature freely show itself. Only then will you be able to show who you really are underneath your tough exterior.

Even if your life has more in common with Penninah, God is still your creator and father and longs for you to recognise this and to come to him. This will enable you to realise the real person he created you to be. The negative experiences that you have endured were designed to help you grow and develop strength and knowledge. These will further develop your character and your ability to make a difference for God's kingdom.

I pray that you will realise that you do not have to be defeated by your past. You are meant to grow and to move forward in spite of it. The quicker you are able to accept what happened to you and then leave it in the past where it belongs, the quicker you will be able to walk into the destiny you were created for.

Bev Thomas-Graham

Finally, you can move on

We are reliably told that God never gives us more than we can bear, and this is true. He alone knows what our thresholds are and how far they can be stretched.

When you feel like giving up because it seems there is just no way you can go on, you may find that your situation does not get any better right away. This may be because God knows that if you can be pushed just a little more, you will develop even greater endurance skills. This means that the pressure will not let up until you reach the level that God thinks you can reach. Once you understand that this is probably a period of training and preparation for what is ahead, you will find the strength and courage to go on.

You can make a decision to pick yourself up right now. Take on board what you have just read and choose to walk into your destiny. You are not defeated; you are in training, and you cannot move on from this lesson until you learn it. Understand that this is not the picture of your entire life but rather is just a phase right now. Ask God to help you get through it. Ask him to show you mercy so that you can learn what you need to do, and then get out there and do it!

When you start including him in the process, you will very quickly discover reservoirs of strength that you never knew existed within you. He will also cover you with his peace and his love. God wants to use people who are pliable and willing to be used. He cannot use someone who is weak and gives up easily. He wants to know that when he blesses you and puts you in charge of his work, you will rely on him in everything and will totally surrender to his will. You will know that in the midst of chaos, he is the master, and he will

Just Want to be Loved for Me...

orchestrate everything towards his own glory. You will learn to stand still and allow him to act in the situation. This is a powerful place to be, and this is your future.

There is a Hannah inside of you waiting to get out. This is where you will find peace in your life and personal fulfilment. As you understand who God is and what his plans are for your life, you will be empowered to go on.

I know right now you are probably making every excuse under the sun as to why this is not the right time for you to make any changes. Maybe your experiences have hardened you and made you unwilling to take a chance. Be aware that the longer you leave it the harder it will become.

There is no coincidence in you reading this today. God is talking to you right now; you know you cannot go on the way you have been. You are fed up and you want things to change. Well, they can! All you have to do is ask him, and then slowly allow the process to begin. There is a bright future ahead of you and you need to take the first step towards it. Be blessed as you take that step right now... in Jesus' name!

Chapter Five

Just Want to Be Loved for Me...

Leah's Story

Introduction

The twenty-first century woman longs for love and acceptance in the same way that any woman does. Despite the pressure she faces in these modern times to be an icon of independence and self sufficiency, the average woman still longs for her innermost needs to be filled. These needs were built into her at her creation. They also form the basis of how she will experience everything in life.

Subconsciously, we all make choices based on how we think we can achieve acceptance and love. None of us wants to be loved for what we have or what we can do. We are smart enough to know that these things are fleeting and will only last a while. True love is embodied in someone's acceptance of who we really are as a person, and it definitely stands the test of time. True love is demonstrated when we love others unconditionally irrespective of their choices or mistakes – when we love them just as they are.

In modern days, this kind of love is rare and is more commonly found in the relationship between a parent and his or her child. This is an unconditional form of love that surpasses any form of logic or reasoning. It is a pure love based on the bond and relationship between the parent and child. You may be unhappy with the choices your child makes and you may not like them at certain times of their life, but underneath it all you still love them, and there is nothing they can do that's so bad that you will eventually not be able to forgive them for it. It has become harder and harder to find this kind of love and acceptance within a marriage or intimate relationship. Yet, it is the one thing we all search for, and we seek it in order to validate who we are. As King Solomon stated so wisely, there is nothing new under the sun. The Bible is still contemporary and has nuggets of wisdom and truths that are relevant for the way we live today.

In this chapter, I want to talk about the story of Leah and how she coped with her situation. You can read her full story in the book of Genesis chapter 29. But first we need to step back in time to learn a little about Jacob.

The story begins

When we are first introduced to Jacob in the Old Testament, we are told of his plans to leave home. He is going on a journey to see his uncle Laban who lives in Padanaram. He is being sent there to take a wife from within his mother's family. Jacob is free to be with whoever he wants. However, he has been strongly warned that he must not take a wife from the daughters of Canaan, who also live in that land. This is because they have a different religion and their belief systems were steeped in pagan worship. They also had other social customs that deeply contravened the rules of Jacob's own beliefs.

Jacob had a questionable character, and some may even call him a bit of a rogue. His name means 'deceiver', which suits him well. In fact, he had recently just deceived his elder brother Esau out of his birthright. This caused Jacob's father to bless him richly instead of Esau, who should have been blessed as the firstborn.

Jacob's leaving is well timed; his brother is so angry with him that his parents fear that he will be seriously harmed if he doesn't go. This trip is important in more ways than one. It will put some distance between the brothers, and this will

Just Want to be Loved for Me...

hopefully allow things to cool down between them. Jacob will also have to meet and deal with many different kinds of people, some of whom will be every bit as questionable as he is. This will provide the perfect opportunity for him to grow up and fulfil his destiny.

This journey marks a very important period in Jacob's life. One night while on his way, he has an important dream in which God reaffirms his promise to bless his people. This is in line with the very promise he gave to Jacob's father and grandfather, Abraham and Isaac, before him. So we know that God has a very special purpose for Jacob in the future.

When he arrives at his destination, the very first person he meets is a beautiful young lady called Rachel. He meets her as she comes to water her father's sheep by a well. He is struck immediately by how young and beautiful she is, and how gracefully she carries out her duties.

He decides to help her, feeling strangely drawn to her. As he does so, he strikes up a conversation. He is amazed to find that she is very easy going and pleasant to talk to. Within a short time, they find out that they have so much in common. He loves the way she smiles. As the conversation progresses, her initial shyness and one-word replies give way to a more natural way of speaking. Rachel openly asks Jacob about himself and is very interested to hear about his life. It is almost as if time stands still as they talk together. They have covered so many subjects in such a short time. They have joked, laughed, swapped life stories and sympathised with each other all at once. It is as if they have known each other their whole lives.

Jacob notices her fine features and her slender body as she moves around watering the camels. This combined with her charming personality is everything Jacob has hoped to find in a wife. Jacob is definitely attracted to Rachel, and he cannot bear the thought of leaving the well and never seeing her again. He knows he does not want this to be just a one-off meeting with no chance of ever seeing her again.

When she is finished watering the camels, Rachael begins to gather her things to leave. The animals are full now, and it is time to head back home. Jacob is filled with an overwhelming sense of panic. He does not want to say goodbye to Rachel. Even as he thinks this, he realizes how crazy it seems. However, there is something so special about Rachel, and he is drawn to her in a way that he cannot explain. Yes, he is in a strange land and he has no friends yet, and of course, there is the possibility that he will meet more people eventually, but he is reluctant to let go of the first kind person he has met, not to mention the sweetest and most beautiful woman that has ever crossed his path.

He begins to question her about her family. Veiled within polite conversation is his motive of hoping to be able to find her again. He is very pleasantly surprised to find out that he does not have to say goodbye to her at the well after all. Rachel has just told him that her father's name is Laban, and this is exactly who he is on his way to see. Jacob follows Rachel home, and once there, he is immediately welcomed by her whole family.

Settling in a new land

Jacob initially spends time finding his feet in this new land. Everything seems so strange and yet so familiar at

Just Want to be Loved for Me...

the same time. He feels safe with this family, and this gives him the confidence to boldly explore his new surroundings. After Jacob has been a part of Laban's household for about a month, Laban offers Jacob a job and asks him what he would like as wages. There is only one thing Jacob has on his mind, and nothing else will do. This seems to be the perfect opportunity to make a move. Jacob wastes no time in asking for Rachel's hand in marriage.

This seems to be a match made in heaven, and unlike in modern times, it was quite common for cousins to marry each other. Laban heartily agrees but decides that Jacob will have to work for seven years to earn Rachel as his bride. It is a price Jacob is happy to pay, especially because he knows that Rachel has already given him her heart. Their friendship has really blossomed over the last month. They have spent as much time together as they have been allowed (or have dared) to do. There are certain rules that Rachael has to follow, and this means that she cannot be too obvious in talking to him or being with him in public. But he knows that she adores him as much as he adores her, and so they both look forward to the time when they can be joined as husband and wife.

After the seven long years are over, Jacob is ready to claim his prize. He has been looking forward to this day for so long and now he will finally be able to have Rachel as his bride. His love for her has surely stood the test of time. He loves her with all his heart, and this love has kept him going whenever he has felt lonely or fed up and wanted to quit. Just seeing her smile melts his heart and lifts his mood, and he knows he could never refuse her anything.

Rachel is very aware of the impact she has on him, and she often teases him and plays around with him. This embarrasses him, especially if there are other family members around, but it secretly pleases him too, as she can do no wrong in his eyes. Jacob is a faithful man and would never do anything to jeopardise the arrangement he has made with Rachel's father. Rachel also feels secure in Jacob's love for her, and feels so fortunate that she will be able to marry a man that she already loves with all her heart and not just marry someone chosen for her. This is the perfect relationship, and she knows it will only get better. She looks forward to their future together with eagerness and hopeful anticipation.

The wedding

The day of the wedding arrives and Jacob is overcome with excitement and anticipation. The long wait is finally over; at last, he and Rachel can be man and wife. The wedding preparations have been the talk of the town. In fact, everybody is anxious for the wedding to be over and done with so that they can get back to the daily routine of their lives and conduct business as usual. There has been so much to do, to organise and to prepare.

As the day dawns, frantic last-minute adjustments are made, and finally, the women are happy that everything has been done properly and all is in place. Jacob is ready, and he is waiting for them to call to him to take his place at the ceremony.

The wedding begins and the bride arrives. As is customary, the bride is brought to join Jacob at his side, veiled appropriately as the chaste virgin that she is. According

Just Want to be Loved for Me...

to their custom, there will be no public displays of wanton behaviour. She will be quiet, humble and modest.

Today is the happiest day of Jacob's life. He manages to find a few quiet moments to himself to think about his life. He carries out a mental review of both the good and the bad times. He looks around the room and sees all his family and friends who have come to witness the event and to celebrate with him. He is so proud, but at the same time, he is sad that his own parents are not there to share this joyous occasion with him.

He remembers his mother especially. She was always there for him through the good times and the bad, and he misses her so much. He remembers her beautiful smiling face, her warmth and the comfort of her loving hugs. She would have been so proud of him on this day. He was sure that she would love and adore Rachel just the same as he did. He shook his head and forced the memories and thoughts far back into the recesses of his mind. He blinked hard several times to banish away the tears that threatened to spill out onto his rosy cheeks. He pushed back his shoulders and stood tall. He reasoned with himself to stay strong. There was no point in dwelling on the past. This was his life now, and he must make the best of it.

Jacob glanced over at Rachael and wondered how she was feeling in this moment of anticipation. She sat straight-backed and taut, with her head slightly bowed. She appeared to be concentrating on what the rabbi was saying to them now. She never looked in Jacob's direction, and he knew that this was probably because she was nervous. Jacob wished that he could offer her a smile and reassure her that everything would be alright, and that once they got through the strict rituals of the ceremony, they could look forward to a happy life together. She looked so grown up and serious, unlike the light-hearted young woman he knew. Still, once the ceremony was over they would have their whole lives together. He smiled to himself as he pictured how cute she would look, blushing and grinning with embarrassment when he teased her about this later. Most of all he looked forward to being able to hold her in his arms.

Jacob felt sympathetic toward her because he knew that weddings were always such a stressful event for women. So much was expected of Rachel, and she would be completely exhausted by the time they joined hands in matrimony. She most likely would have attended to the constant changes and preparations right up to the last minute. Rachael, like most women, would have dreamed of her wedding day from a very young age. Every detail would have been meticulously planned, with nothing left to chance.

Once their wedding ceremony was over, the festivities began. There was a palpable sense of excitement in the air as everyone joined in the celebrating. There were many different dishes of food to eat and untold amounts of wine to drink. This was a time for merrymaking, dancing and singing. It was also the time when the close family of women would get together to offer Rachel their advice and support. They would make jokes and give her last minute tips and advice as she approached her wedding night. This was an important ritual, as it eased the pressure and anxiety she most likely was feeling as she anticipated her first night together with Jacob. For his part, Jacob had hardly seen Rachel after the wedding ceremony because the other women had kept her so occupied.

Just Want to be Loved for Me...

At the end of all of this merrymaking, the bride and groom were escorted to a specially prepared bedchamber, darkened for modesty reasons. It was here that they would spend their first night together as man and wife and consummate their union.

Jacob had been drinking all night, unable to escape as all the men in the village approached him wanting to congratulate him on his wedding and to drink with him. By now, the drink had made him slightly tipsy, but it had thankfully also diminished his nerves. He felt calmer now and was anxious to see his bride. He was also deeply excited because soon he would at last hold Rachel in his arms as his wife.

The aftermath

In the morning, tragedy strikes as Jacob realises with dismay that the woman in his arms is not his beloved Rachel but her older sister Leah. You can imagine his shock and horror at this discovery after spending a night thinking he was with Rachel. He rubs his eyes in disbelief and desperately rifles through his memory, searching for clues from the night before. His heart beats faster and faster and his mind goes into overdrive as he frantically tries to work out what happened.

How could he have been fooled in this way? As he looks at Leah lying there sleeping peacefully next to him, his heart is not softened toward her as it would have been toward Rachel, his true love. He shakes Leah roughly and demands an explanation. She is jolted out of a deep sleep, and it takes her a moment to remember where she is. Remembering the sweet intimacy of the night before, she reaches out languidly to hold Jacob but feels a deep sense of rejection as he recoils from her in anger. He asks her repeatedly what she is doing there in his bed, pretending to be the woman he intended to marry.

Jacob feels as though he is losing his mind. He is suffering from shock and disappointment, and has a million questions that need answering immediately. He has given up on getting any answers from Leah. He leaves her sitting up in bed, her head bowed and resting on her knees, which are drawn up under her chin, her arms hugging her legs in a pose of self-protection. She still has not offered a single word of explanation. Even when Jacob demands an answer, she simply raises her head for a second and then promptly lowers it again. It is long enough for him to see that her eyes are red and puffy, numbed of any emotion. He also sees the silent tears coursing down her cheeks. Each tear speaks volumes of how she is feeling right now.

Her tears do not move Jacob, but instead they only add to the anger and turmoil he feels. Jacob storms out of the room, and with each angry stride, he calls out for Rachel. He is desperate to find her now and begins to panic when she does not respond.

When Jacob confronts his father in law, Laban, he is mortified to find that he is unrepentant. Laban tells Jacob that he should have known that it is almost impossible to marry the younger daughter off first, and therefore it should be no surprise to him that he was forced to marry Leah. In Leah's case, if she had not been married first, it would have been even harder for her to find a husband because she was very different from Rachel in ways that made her a bit less attractive to men: She was quieter and more timid, and

Just Want to be Loved for Me...

she was rather plain looking. Rachel was always the more beautiful and outgoing one, and men were generally more attracted to her.

Jacob was unable to comprehend what he was hearing from Laban, who was justifying his actions as if it was the most normal thing in the world for him to have tricked Jacob into marrying Leah. For his part, Jacob was only now experiencing the sickening realisation that this had all been planned beforehand and that he had been completely deceived by Laban.

It is hard for us to imagine that Jacob would not have figured out on the wedding night that he had been tricked. On the other hand, considering that the wedding night was conducted in a darkened bedchamber, why on earth would he ever suspect that the woman he held in his arms and made love to was not the one he had contracted to marry?

I have often wondered whether Jacob and Leah spoke to each other at any point during the night. Surely, if they had conversed, the deception would have been discovered much earlier on.

Another reason why it seems hard to imagine that such deception could occur is because Rachael and Jacob knew each other really well. They had lived almost like family members, in terms of being around each other every day. Their relationship had been bonded by love and friendship, so it seems almost inconceivable that Jacob wouldn't have sensed somehow that the woman lying next to him wasn't Rachel.

But one thing we must consider in the framework of their culture is that their wedding night was the first time they were taking things a step further and connecting with each other intimately. It would have been normal and even natural for them both to feel a little awkward and embarrassed or even shy with each other. If Jacob did indeed murmur sweet nothings to the woman in his arms, he would not have been surprised by her silence or her faint, barely audible sounds. Young women can be very shy as new brides, especially if they are inexperienced and anxious. They are often filled with worry that their husband may not like what he finds underneath their clothes. A young bride often worries that she will not please her new husband.

In the case of Rachel and Leah, it is also possible that the two sisters were of a similar size, shape and weight. Jacob therefore would not have noticed that the veiled woman by his side at the wedding wasn't Rachel. In any event, there was no reason for it to enter his mind that he was being duped.

So what was to happen now? Laban insists that Jacob must stay married to Leah in order to honour his marriage vows to her. Laban also insists that Jacob must now commit to working another seven years if he still wants Rachel to be his wife. The only positive aspect of this situation is that he can take Rachel as his wife now instead of waiting until the end of the period.

Despite being angry and very upset, Jacob's intentions have not changed. He is still in love with Rachel and wants her to be his wife. His bargaining power is limited and he knows it. If he refuses to keep Leah, then Laban may well decide to marry off Rachel to someone else. This would not

Just Want to be Loved for Me...

prove to be so hard because Rachel was an excellent catch for any man. Laban would not have to resort to cunning means to find her a husband as he had done with Leah.

Jacob reluctantly decides not to upset the apple cart. He focuses on the prize ahead and agrees to do as his father in law asks. It is funny to see the old adage 'what goes around comes around' come into play. At the start of the story, we see Jacob as the cunning and deceitful one who tricks his brother into giving up his birthright. Now we see that Jacob has met his match in his Uncle Laban, whose cunning behaviour is similar to Jacob's behaviour with his brother Esau. Now Jacob knows firsthand how painful it is to want something so badly and then to have it taken away so cruelly. He also knows what it is like to be at the mercy of someone else and not be able to do much about it.

The love triangle begins

So here we have the start of a love triangle between Jacob, Leah and Rachel. As the story unfolds, we see how human nature intervenes at every point to create discomfort, rivalry and jealousy between the two women. Jacob is caught in the middle and must strive to keep the peace between them.

Every time I study this Bible story, I am drawn to the predicament faced by Leah. As the eldest daughter, it would have been very difficult for her to live in the shadow of her younger, prettier and physically more attractive sister. As women, we all want to be loved and accepted for who we are. It must have been so difficult for Leah as she struggled to find a place in the family where *she* was the one who was special, loved and adored, and whose behaviour was considered cute or quaint. Sadly for Leah, these compliments were given to Rachael quite regularly while she (Leah) had to stand by and smile politely as if it didn't hurt that no one complimented her in that manner. It had also been painful for Leah to watch the endless parade of suitors asking for Rachel's hand in marriage because she was so pretty, popular and outgoing.

Leah was the one with the weak eye that everyone knew about. This made her less confident about herself, and she often wondered if she would ever end up with a normal life, which naturally meant being happily married and the mother of many children. Her mother may have compensated Leah for her lack of physical beauty by raising her with other skills that could be used to overcome her physical shortcomings. She may have been equipped with good housekeeping or good parenting skills. Her mother may have taught her other practical things that she could use to impress a man looking for a good wife. This may have included learning how to dance or learning the art of how to successfully seduce and please a man.

It is interesting to note that Jacob was first required to wait seven years before he could even consider marrying Rachel, his intended bride. This would have given Laban more than enough time to find a suitable husband for Leah. It did not happen, though, and as the end of the seven-year period grew closer, the pressure was on. If Laban could not find a suitable husband for his eldest daughter, the consequences would be dire if he let the youngest marry first. Once Rachel was married, there would be little chance that Leah would ever be married. Leah would face a life of being single and would never be able to become a wife and mother. She would face the future as an old maid. Her ability to live out her elder years in comfortable old age

Just Want to be Loved for Me...

would be uncertain, and she would be forced to live on the charity and goodwill of others.

There is no doubt that Laban committed an act of treachery in tricking Jacob into marrying Leah. However, he would have been driven by the tenderness of a father's love. He wanted nothing more than to make sure that both his daughters were cared for and that their future would be secured after he was gone. He would have used this argument to secure the acceptance of both girls in carrying out the plan. They would have both clearly understood in simple terms that the choice was ultimately not theirs. Their loyalty to the family would have been called upon. They would have been told that they had to put the needs of the whole family first.

In spite of her love for Jacob, this was not a time for Rachel to be selfish and to think of her own happiness. If she did, she would condemn her sister to a cruel and miserable existence. There is no way she could have done that. Rachael reluctantly agreed to the plan. Her heart was broken and her dreams of an idyllic life with Jacob had been cruelly dashed and taken away. Life was just not fair.

She grieved in private for the loss of the happy married life with him that she had so looked forward to, and as the bitter tears fell unchecked onto her pillow she cried out to God and prayed for the strength to see things through. Although her heart ached unbearably and she had difficulty in staying focussed, she managed to pull herself together enough to play her role as the dutiful daughter and sister. She managed to keep away from Jacob in the days and weeks leading up to the marriage ceremony and she was duly available to help to make the wedding plan work.

It must also have been so soul destroying for Leah to grow up in her younger sister's shadow, and then to be forced to look on as Jacob committed himself to working for her father for seven long years to earn Rachel's hand. She must have dreamed that one day someone would look at her with the same longing and tenderness, and love her enough to make such a commitment to her. She could only dream what it was like to have a man whose heart would melt in her presence, and who would love her so much that he would find himself unable to deny her anything her heart desired. During the entire seven-year waiting period she had clung on to this hope, even up until the wedding day itself.

By this time, Leah would have known Jacob really well. She also would have been aware of his particular likes and dislikes. She would have grown accustomed to watching him and Rachel interact together as they became closer than friends. It was plain for all to see that they adored each other. Leah also would have noticed the secret looks between them, and she would have known how much they both longed for the day when they could be together.

A woman's love

Things were about to get ugly for Leah; soon she would be placed in a position where she would have no option but to obey her father's wishes. If she refused, her future would become very unstable. She had always secretly admired and loved Jacob anyhow, and she **had** to go along with her father's plan to make the best of a bad situation and to secure her future.

Just Want to be Loved for Me...

In her heart, she fervently hoped that once Jacob got to know her properly as his wife, he would grow to love her in the same way that he loved Rachel. She prayed that she would be able to appeal to him on a personal level, and that she could be the best wife he could have ever had. She knew that he was sensible and appreciated good things. This would surely work in her stead. He would soon forget the disappointment he had first felt when he realised that he had been deceived into marrying her.

She remembered their wedding night ... ah, the bliss of those intimate moments when he took her in his arms and kissed her so tenderly at first and then more passionately as he made love to her. He had awoken her own passions, and her own personal love for him grew as her body shyly responded to him. For that night, she was his prize, his princess and the apple of his eye. When their passion was spent and they lay in one another's arms afterward, she exulted in the feeling of being a woman at last, and now she was **his** wife. She had truly given him her all and they had become one flesh as man and wife. She was convinced that she had made the right decision and that everything would work out perfectly. Surely now he would love her.

You can imagine the impact on her when all hell broke loose the next day. She had become so lost in the passion of the night before that she had forgotten for a moment that Jacob had thought he was making love to Rachel and not her. Jacob despised her now and was very angry. Leah had already heard of the new deal that had been made between Jacob and her father. She was utterly stunned to learn that Jacob was willing to work for a further seven years for Rachel. Leah would also have realised by now (and with a sinking heart, no less) that Jacob did not love her or want her. He would only stay married to her to please her father and to ensure that he would in the end get the woman he really loved – her sister Rachel. It was always about Rachel.

This could have been the end of the marriage, but Leah had tasted what a real marriage could be like, and even though this situation was not ideal, she was not about to give up this prize husband she had won, albeit by default. She was haunted by the bittersweet memories of her wedding night. Their lovemaking had been so real and so special, and her womanly intuition knew that he had enjoyed it too. She hurt deeply to think that it did not mean anything to him at all now.

In her mind, she had convinced herself that surely Jacob knew that it was not Rachel he had held that night, and yet he had continued to make love to her, Leah, knowing this full well. After all, he knew her well enough to know the shape and size of her body and to pick up on the various other aspects of her personality that should have revealed the truth to him.

Anyhow, what was done was done, and there was no turning back now. Jacob kept his word and remained her husband, but there was a difference between them now. He could barely conceal his lack of feeling for her. Although she continued to make love to him with all her heart, she couldn't help but notice that he only functionally performed his duties as a husband. She longed for it to be the same as it was on their wedding night, but that level of intimacy and passion was never present between them again. She never gave up hope, nonetheless. She was a woman of courage and strength, and she took her vows seriously. She would make this relationship work at all cost.

Just Want to be Loved for Me...

Leah also had to live with the fact that Rachel was now Jacob's wife as well, and she burned with envy each time she saw them together. She was under no illusion of the deep love they shared. She could only hope and pray that if she could turn things around somehow, then just maybe she would one day experience that same love again. In the meantime, despite being married and settled on the face of it, she was lonely; she deeply longed for intimacy and love.

Leah turned to God in the midst of her distress and he heard her prayer. He opened up her womb and began to bless her with children. At the same time, God shut Rachel's womb, and although she received Jacob's unconditional love, she was not able to honour him by bearing his children. This caused her untold misery and pain. There seemed to be no winners in this complicated situation.

Finding fulfilment as a mother

By understanding the meaning of the names that Leah chose for her children, we are able to see where she was emotionally and spiritually at different stages of her life. In her part of the world and in Biblical times especially, names were very important, as they always had a meaning or message. Thus, they were always chosen with great thought and care.

Her first child was a son whom she called Reuben, because God knew of her affliction. She was still filled with the hope that her husband would love her, especially now that she had given him his first-born child and a male heir. Sadly, things did not change, and she had another son who she called Simeon, which means 'hearing'. This was because she knew that God had heard that she was hated and that Jacob preferred Rachel to her. Again, she was filled with hope that having this child would bridge the gap between Jacob and her, but it didn't. She called her third son Levi, which means 'joined'. This is because she believed that her husband would surely be joined to her now that she had borne him three sons.

When she had her fourth son, she called him Judah, which means 'praise', because she wanted to praise God for all her blessings. She was now trying to face the fact that God's will must be done in her life, even if it meant that her situation would never change; or, if it would, maybe the time was not yet right. She remembered that in all things we must offer praise to God. Often times this is the hardest thing to do when you are hurt or disappointed. When you are in a situation where you have no more control over what happens, offering praise often helps to bring you through it. God is drawn to us as we offer praises to him, especially when we are in the midst of trouble. Praise is often the vehicle through which a breakthrough will come. Sadly for Leah, she was unable to have any more children after this.

The competition heats up

Rachel at this point was beside herself with distress at not having any children at all, so she gave her maid to Jacob so that she could act as a surrogate. Bilhah, the maid, bore two sons that would be counted as belonging to Rachel and Jacob.

Leah is now so jealous that sons have been born to them, and through a maid, no less, that she decides to take things into her own hands. She is not yet ready to give up the fight for her husband's love and feels that she has lost her edge in being the only wife to bear him sons. She gives her maid, Zilpah, to Jacob, and she bears him two more sons to add to the total number of Leah's children. The rivalry and competition between Leah and Rachel heats up and is not over yet. Meanwhile, their relationship sinks to an all time low. They are almost like sworn enemies, and there is such a barrier between them that it creates tension for the whole family.

Seeing all of this, God decides to show mercy to Leah again, and she has two more sons, Issachar and Zebulon, and a daughter whom she names Dinah (the same Dinah we learned about in chapter two).

Still no love for Leah

Even after all of this, things still do not change for Leah. By now, she has spent the greatest part of her life longing to be loved and accepted by the man she has shared her life and heart with. She has done everything in her power to turn things around, hoping beyond hope that with each new son she bears, Jacob will recognise her at last as his most beloved wife. Sons were very important for families at that time and were prized more highly than daughters were. This means that Leah's contribution as a fertile child-bearer of sons should have been highly valued. However, with each new son came fresh disappointment that things still had not changed. She has grown weary from her efforts, and she has almost lost the will to live.

She realises in the depths of her spirit that she must accept things as they are. It is a lesson that comes too little and too late. She has almost been completely destroyed by her experience. She now knows that if someone does not love you the way you are, there is nothing you can do to make them love you. Love is a spontaneous emotion or it may grow over an extended period, but this can only happen where there is mutual respect to start with. In Leah's case, her relationship with Jacob was based on deception and dishonesty from the very beginning, and she feels that nothing good can come out of it.

The rivalry ends

Finally, God mercifully opens up Rachel's womb and she gives birth to a son called Joseph. This brings her much joy and causes her relationship with Jacob to grow even closer still. Soon after Joseph is born, Rachel is thrilled to find that she is pregnant again, and she looks forward to growing her own family with Jacob. After a protracted and painful labour, she finally gives birth to another son whom she names Benjamin. Sadly, her body gives up after the sheer strain of the ordeal. She dies leaving the two boys behind.

For Leah's part, watching her younger sister suffer and die in childbirth finally quells the jealousy she has carried in her heart all these years. She is filled with a mixture of grief for the loss of her sister and an awkward sense of relief at the same time. She can finally now, allow herself to remember the sisterly love, affection and close relationship they once shared. She had become so used to hiding any emotions she may have had once they had become rivals. They had barely spoken to each for years and everyone knew there was no love lost between them. The situation caused by their affections for Jacob remained a firm barrier between them, now finally broken by death. Silent tears fall unbidden as she reminisces over Rachel's life and death. She remembers her

Just Want to be Loved for Me...

vividly as images of her life flashed before her like a silent film. Her sweet sister was no more. She would never again hear her infectious laughter as she teased and played with all the children. There would be no more chances to make up or to fix the relationship between them. Leah grieved for the loss of the little girl she always fiercely protected as the older sister, when they were small. She cried fresh tears as she remembered how much she had missed out on while they were rivals and how powerless they both were to change their situation.

Jacob's family has now increased to twelve sons and a daughter. The sons would go on to form the twelve tribes of Israel and play a crucial role in the history and development of their people.

Leah had finally managed to fulfil her role as Jacob's only true wife in spite of what she had been through to get there. Now that the rivalry had ended both Leah and Jacob live out the rest of their lives peacefully together. It is strange to realise that she would be the one to be honoured as Jacob's wife in the end. It was Leah who was buried with him in the family tomb in the field of Mach-Pelah in Canaan, which was originally bought by Abraham. She was laid to rest with him and his forefathers.

Jacob's beloved Rachel was buried in Bethlehem where they were living at the time of her death. Jacob laid a special pillow upon her grave there in memory of his first and only true love.

In this sad story, we see the inner torment of a woman who has spent her whole life in search of being loved and accepted. Leah tried so hard, using every means at her disposal, to turn around a situation that began badly and continued in the same vein. She gave Jacob many fine healthy sons that would make him the envy of other fathers around him. She was the best wife she could be and yet none of it was ever enough.

The Leah type

This story touches my heart in so many ways because in my own lifetime I have seen so many Leah types: women who spend a large portion of their time trying to please their man and never quite being able to do so. This may come in many forms. It may be that they have to forsake their families or drop their friends because he demands this of them. Somewhere along the line, they have become afraid that if they displease him he will walk away. This means that they are not free to be themselves or to stand up to him. This causes many women to live in complete fear of what may happen if their men leave them.

In other cases, after a woman is through giving of herself and surrendering her will to her man, she decides to take things a step further. She then acts under the misapprehension that if she gives him a child – a living symbol and embodiment of their lovemaking – then that will seal their relationship.

Women with this mindset are unable to see that when things are not right in a relationship, a child will not bring solutions. In a lot of cases, a child brings added strain and pressure as the couple are forced to work together to support the child and to ensure that its needs are put first. In many cases, the strain of parenthood becomes instrumental in finally breaking the relationship down. The couple walk

Just Want to be Loved for Me...

away from one another but are then forced to remain in each other's lives, to a certain extent, for the sake of the child.

Now things begin to take an ugly turn as both of them struggle to move on with their lives trying to forget their painful past. This is not always as easy to manage as they think it will be. In every situation they will each face in life, they will be forced to consider the child and each other. Every decision will be impacted in this manner. The child may even be used as a bargaining tool to control or exert influence over the other partner. In the worst cases, children may even be used as a means of disrupting new relationships or making unreasonable demands on the former partner. Either way it is a recipe for disaster.

Quite often we see women who have experienced the Leah dilemma more than once, and they end up with three or four children, all of whom have different fathers. This is typical of women who are determined to never stop looking for that perfect partner. They may also still be on a mission to find the love they so desperately need in general, love that could be met by their heavenly Father if they would let Him. So many women search for a 'good man' to fill that internal emptiness and longing that has left them dissatisfied and fed up with life. This is because they innately feel unable to fulfil the primary purposes that they were made for. So they keep on trying with each new man, refusing to see the pattern as the same scenes unfold over and over again in their lives. They are hoping beyond hope that this time it will be different. They find themselves wanting so desperately to break the cycle, but they are never quite sure how to do it.

Like Leah, they too will reach a point where they are worn down. They will finally realise that it may never happen for them and that they need to find another way to fulfil their purpose. Sadly, by this time they are hurt, broken and bitter, always looking over the past and wondering how they could have changed it and what they could have or should have done differently. There are no easy answers, and coping with this kind of deeply entrenched regret sometimes leads to a sense of hopelessness and despair.

Be encouraged

I was encouraged by Leah's story, particularly how she chose to cope with her difficult situation. She was a woman of courage and strength. She never gave up, and she used her relationship with God to see her through some of the most difficult times of her life.

Each child she bore was named in line with her relationship with God at the time of that child's birth. It is interesting to note that she gave her fourth child a name that means 'praise'. She accepted that God had heard her prayer, and she chose to see her sons as a blessing God gave to her in the midst of a very bad situation. She knew that God cared about her, and she had accepted that as her creator, he had a plan for her life. She totally trusted him and handed over her situation to him when things didn't seem to be going her way. Even when, on the face of it, her prayers remained unanswered, she still chose to give him praise.

We are told that her womb closed up after this, but God still remembered her and continued to hear her prayers. When it looked like it was all over for her as the competition

Just Want to be Loved for Me...

raged on, God mercifully opened her womb again and allowed her to have three more children.

Modern Leahs

As you've read about Leah's touching life story, if you've found yourself thinking, *I'm a Leah*, I encourage you to take hope from how she handled her situation. On the face of it, we modern women seem to have more choices than Leah had, particularly concerning the direction that our lives can take. You would often not know it, though, when you see that women today find themselves equally unable to break away from a loveless relationship that is stifling them. There may be social, economic and cultural reasons that cause their difficulties. Far more often, it is the fear factor. There is a real fear that they may lose the chance to change things if they give up the loveless relationship.

The terrible truth is that if this relationship has been going on for a long time, there is little chance that it will actually change by itself. There is the loneliness you feel each night as you struggle to fall asleep next to someone who has cheated on you. Or it may be that your partner shows little or no interest in you and has other things going on that clearly do not include you. This situation will slowly eat away at you until every ounce of your self-respect, dignity and pride have been eroded.

Many women regularly go through an emotional autopsy while they're in a bad relationship. They go over the events in the relationship again and again in their minds in a ritual of painful self-recrimination, hoping each time to find the reason why their partner shows no interest in them anymore. They often blame themselves and dream up new ways of adjusting their behaviour or responses to situations in the hope that it will ignite a familiar spark of interest or rekindle the love.

Some women find themselves craving sex all the time as a way to feel loved. This eventually irritates their partner who begins to feel like a sex object. He may continuously reject her when she tries to initiate intimacy with him. This has the uncomfortable effect of leaving her feeling even more dejected and forlorn.

Contrary to popular opinion, this renewed interest in intimacy is not the result of a heightened libido or a sign that the woman has suddenly become sex crazed. Too often, women in these situations find that the only time they have the full attention of their partner is when the two of them are making love.

For a few moments, she is the most important thing in his world. As she lays there in his arms, she sees him at his most vulnerable, and she remembers better times. He may even offer words of endearment or express his need for her at that moment. For a short while, she hopes that the lovemaking will act as a trigger and remind him of better times. She hopes that it will rekindle the emotions of the past. All too soon, though, it is over and things go back to normal. The moment is lost and the feeling of being the most precious thing in his life is gone until the next time they make love.

When a woman craves sex for this reason, what she actually craves is her partner's time and attention. When she finds herself pregnant with his child, she again feels like the most precious person in his world. She is carrying his child, a living by-product of the love and union they shared in a moment of intimacy. She has been chosen as a vessel to bring forth the next generation of his seed. When this is done in the correct way, the man will experience an innate tenderness and desire to protect the woman carrying his child. He will stand tall with his shoulders back and his chest puffed out, emanating a sense of pride and achievement.

The woman will revel in this and will carry herself with pride at the precious gift she is carrying. Sometimes a woman will also desperately want a child to replace what she feels is missing in her relationship. This is all about meeting her own emotional needs. She knows that the child will depend on her and need her unconditionally. This will go a long way toward filling the emptiness she feels inside. It is, however, a short-lived triumph, as raising a child on your own, or even within a troubled relationship, brings a whole new set of difficulties.

The way out

Modern Leahs need to take a lesson from the Biblical Leah. The answer to this predicament is the same today as it was in past days. Only by surrendering yourself to God will you come to a place where you are able to move on from the painful situations you find yourself in.

Many women lose out on precious years when they are in denial of their situation or when they feel unable to move on. Even when they use all kinds of measures to find fulfilment, those eventually lose their savour, and the woman still ends up feeling empty. She may seek fulfilment by immersing herself in work, church or children and by being super efficient. Sometimes she may choose to dedicate her life to serving others as a carer, helper or nurturer. All of these things are a desperate inner cry for love and acceptance. There is an overwhelming feeling of wanting to be needed, and of needing to make a difference in somebody's life. This leads to anger, frustration and rejection, usually because, having done all they are able to do, others still seem ungrateful of their efforts or even turn their backs on them at a moment's notice.

True inner peace comes only from one source. There is no alternative and there is no compromise. You need to make a decision today and stick to it. Break this wretched cycle once and for all. Just like Leah, decide that enough is enough. Whoever you are and whatever your situation, talk to God about it right now. Ask him to intervene and to show you the way out. Surrender it to him and allow ***him*** to lead the way. This is your path in life right now, and you should follow it wholeheartedly and with praise to God.

Focus your attention on him whenever the nagging doubts, fear and worries surface. Just be still and let God do his thing: Let him fix it for you. This will involve a complete mindset change on your part, but you will see things begin to fall in place for you as you apply his word in your life.

What do you have to lose? In the New Testament book of Matthew 6:25, we read that God takes care of everything he creates no matter how small or insignificant it may seem. He takes time out to make sure that every detail is taken care of. The example is given of grass and the flowers that are perfectly created and cared for even though their life span is so short. He doesn't compromise on their design or the quality of their life. He makes time to provide for and to feed the birds even when the weather is harsh and food

Just Want to be Loved for Me...

is scarce. Verse 29 says that even Solomon was not dressed as well as all of these.

Therefore, consider how much more he cares for you. There is no need to worry. In any event, no one is able to change things by worrying anyway. God knows what you need and he will provide for you – he just wants you to trust him and to release it all to him, and to allow him to do his part. Verse 32 instructs us very clearly to seek ***first*** the kingdom of God and his righteousness, and ***then*** all things will be added to us. This takes the stress and responsibility of worrying away from you. To do your part, you must first simply seek him – that's all there is to it. It really is as simple as that. Once you fully understand this, you will feel so relieved and liberated. You will face each new day with hope, strength and faith in your creator.

Don't delay – start today! Release your worries and fears, and then offer your praise to God (sing, dance, clap, pray and read his Word). It's as easy as that – try it with all your heart and watch him begin to work in your life. Then before you know it, you will be so immersed in him that your worries will seem to subside, and one day you may realise that your deliverance has actually arrived. When that day comes, you will be ready to move onward and upward to a higher and more awesome level in him. Now you can finally be in a position to embrace and step forward into your purpose and into the destiny for which he created you.

Chapter Six

A Mother's Love

Rizpah's Story

Introduction – God's love

This chapter is all about the devotion and unconditional love that mothers have towards their children. In many ways, it is only by looking at this relationship that we can truly get a brief insight into the depths of God's love for us. Because a mother's love is unconditional (usually), it mirrors God's love, albeit on a much smaller scale.

In the Bible, we read of how much God loves us. We read of how much he hurts when we hurt and how much he longs for us to choose to love him in return. We also read of the abundance of his mercy, love and grace, and this allows him to forgive us each time we choose to operate outside of his will.

This same love will always welcome us back into the fold, even when we have gone against God and been hurt and beaten by the world as a result. We often only remember him when all of our options are spent or when we are in trouble. We call on his name looking for a quick fix to the problem, only to then forget him as we revert to our old ways again afterwards. Most of us abuse the fact that we know he is always there and is always ready to forgive and help us. We know that he changes not and that he can be relied upon.

It is interesting to contemplate how so many people feel disillusioned and sad because they are so frequently used by others and then 'hung out to dry'. They feel especially cheated because they have given of their time and resources, and have even gone out of their way to help others, with no thanks or appreciation given. Sadly, they find that once the person's crisis is over, they never see or hear from them again. There is no level of appreciation or gratitude for the favour. Even when there is an initial burst of thanks, it seems shallow and perfunctory, and the gratitude itself is short lived.

No one likes to feel used, and we all like to feel valued and loved for who we are. Yet this is exactly how most of us treat God. We know he made us in his image, and therefore we think it is reasonable to assume that he will also have the same feelings we have. We see this in the Bible when we read of God being sad, angry, or hurt, or when he is happy and rejoicing.

A mother's love

What does the Bible have to say about a mother's love? There are many examples in the Bible of women who were wonderful mothers, even in the midst of all kinds of unusual and often difficult situations. In fact, many of the stories are very well known. The Bible talks about mothers such as Sarah, Rachel and Hannah who all found it very difficult to conceive and to bear children. Motherhood became something very precious to them because they had longed for it with all their hearts but they had to be specially blessed in order to become mothers. It didn't happen easily for them as it does with so many women. This heightened the experience for them, causing them to revere the blessing of motherhood even more.

Other women in the Bible were chosen to become mothers to sons who were destined to make a real difference in the lives and history of God's chosen people. These mothers would have struggled with the bittersweet joy of learning that a baby was on its way, only to become emotionally

Just Want to be Loved for Me...

fraught years later as their sons began to walk out of their lives completely and into their destiny as men.

Samson's mother was filled with high hopes for her son who was a special gift to her from God. As a Nazarite, he was destined to be raised up to take his place as one of the judges of Israel bringing strength and leadership to his people. His mother would live to see him walk away from all that to go live with the enemy. He would be tortured, imprisoned and killed along with his enemies. His mother would witness the return of his broken body, which would herald her shattered dreams for her son and break her heart completely.

In the Old Testament, we read of Jochebed, a mother whose love caused her to risk her life to keep her son Moses from being killed at birth. We see her ultimately choosing to give him up to be raised in a foreign household just to preserve his life and to allow him to fulfil his destiny.

Elizabeth, in the New Testament, was delighted to learn that she was carrying a son who would one day become John the Baptist, the one who would lead the way for Jesus, the Messiah. She would later lose her son because of the threat he posed to the local officials, who had him beheaded.

Hannah welcomed the arrival of her son Samuel only to have to give him up to be raised in the temple. This was because of the promise she made to God before he was even conceived. Her love for her son and devotion to God made her fulfil this promise even though it would tear at her heartstrings to let him go.

Rizpah's story

The woman I want to focus on in this chapter is not well known at all. You can read her story in the book of 2 Samuel beginning with chapter 3 all the way through to chapter 21. Her name is Rizpah, and she was one of King Saul's concubines. Her story is one of strength and courage and is an example to all of us of how far a mother will go to protect her family. Here we see the depths of a mother's love, which surpasses all logical and reasonable considerations.

Rizpah was the daughter of Aiah who was a Horite. In the course of her life, there was one fateful day that would change her life forever. It was the day King Saul came to visit her city. Everyone was so excited when the news spread that he was passing through. There were so many stories of him, his men and his many conquests and victories. He was a powerful king, and people were in awe of him, his people and their God. Everyone wanted to get a glimpse of this great man, and so they all rushed to the city to jostle in place for the best vantage point to watch as King Saul rode by with his men.

Rizpah was no different from the others. She was young and curious too, and she wanted to see for herself what all the fuss was about. In any event, everyone else would be there, and it would be a good time to catch up with her friends and to get out of doing chores for the afternoon. People were lined up all along the streets and some had even climbed up to the rooftops to get a better glimpse of Saul as he passed by with his men. Rizpah was unable to see anything as she struggled to get through the crowd hoping to find a small opening to push herself forward. There was a buzz of excitement and expectation, with each person

Just Want to be Loved for Me...

trying to outdo the other with their own tales of Saul and his escapades.

Suddenly she heard her named being called out; as she quickly turned in the direction it was coming from, she saw her friend Huldah gesturing excitedly and calling her over. Huldah had managed to secure herself a very nice spot at the front of the crowd, and she was glad to see that Rizpah had changed her mind and decided to come out to see the procession after all. Now that her destination was secure, Rizpah pushed through the crowds with even more urgency until she finally stood next to Huldah. The two girls giggled together as Huldah teased Rizpah about not wanting to come at first. Huldah knew all there was to know about King Saul, and when she had heard that he was coming to their city, she was the one who could not wait to see him. She was fascinated by all that she had heard and wanted to see if he would live up to the rumours in person.

Rizpah had been bored by all her constant chattering and was only able to muster up a feigned interest. At the last minute though, her curiosity had got the better of her. She got ready in a hurry and made her way out to the crowds gathering along the street, anxious not to miss out on all the excitement. It was not every day that a celebrity came to town, and the visit would be talked about for days afterwards. She didn't want to be left out of all the excitement and have to sit idly by listening to the tales that would be told over and over of this momentous day. She knew that she simply had to go.

The crowds were in good spirits as they joked and laughed with each other to pass the time. Rizpah listened with slight amusement and some pride as Huldah impressed the people standing nearby with her knowledge of Saul. She was such an animated storyteller and she easily made people laugh with her bubbly and humorous tales. By now the crowds were getting so thick that Rizpah and Huldah found themselves being pushed and shoved as more people tried to listen and join in, but mainly to get a glimpse of the oncoming procession. Then there was a ripple of excitement and a sudden forward surge in the crowd as everyone turned to crane their necks to get a better view. Saul was finally here. The crowds cheered and waved as he and his men made their way down the street.

A chance meeting

Huldah grabbed Rizpah's arm and pointed to where the heads of the men were now emerging. There were so many of them it was hard to see who was who, but there was one man who clearly stood out among the rest. Rizpah's smile froze as she saw King Saul come into view. He was so distinctive it was hard not to stare in awe. The rumours were all true. He was so tall that he easily stood head and shoulders above his men, and broad shoulders they were, framing his strong, lean physique. Underneath his helmet, she noticed that his dark hair was thick and wavy. His handsome face was ravaged by worry and a pervading look of weariness, and his kind, dark eyes looked sad.

Rizpah was unable to take her eyes away from him. He was a splendid sight. She watched mesmerised as he made his way closer and closer to where they were standing. In her mind, she fantasised about how it would feel to have those strong arms around her, protecting her, and to have those eyes focused solely on her. More than anything, she wanted to see the sadness in them replaced with endearing love.

Just Want to be Loved for Me...

Mentally she visualised herself running her fingers through his thick wavy hair and gently stroking his temples as he relaxed peacefully in her arms.

She was jolted back to reality as Huldah nudged her in the ribs to tell her that Saul was actually looking in their direction. Rizpah's face burned red as she flushed with embarrassment. She was now ashamed of herself and her wanton thoughts. She was mortified to realise that she had been staring at him and he had seen her. Huldah was waving frantically at him, cheering and egging Rizpah on to do the same. Rizpah was unable to move, and her ears and face burned with the sudden rush of blood that betrayed her excitement.

Unknown to her, it was the very fact that she stood so still in a crowd so filled with excitement that caught the attention of Saul. He noticed how she just stood there in awe watching everything and everyone around her. He saw her large brown eyes mesmerised and trying to drink everything in like a sponge. He noticed her pale creamy complexion in perfect contrast to the dark bouncy curls that framed her face. Underneath her pretty headscarf, the long mound of coiled hair threatened to spill out in protest of being bound up. He strained to see more but couldn't because she was jammed in tight by the crowds. He did, however, notice that beneath her robe, her body looked long and slender, and her perfectly rounded breasts strained against the soft fabric of her dress. She was definitely a beauty, and Saul felt a familiar surge of passion, longing and lust rise up within him. Saul and his men had been on the road for a long time, and his whole body tingled with excitement at the thought of holding a beautiful woman in his arms again.

She was smiling now as her friend pointed at something near Saul. Suddenly without warning, Rizpah threw her head back and laughed. In an instant, Saul froze, and he could swear that he heard her laughter distinctively amidst the crowd. She had perfectly even white teeth framed by her lovely full red lips. Her laughter lit up her whole face and her brown eyes twinkled mischievously. She stopped still as she realised that he too was watching her just as she had watched him, and she blushed red, averted her eyes and looked embarrassed. A moment later, she shyly looked up at him again and their eyes met and held for an instant. Saul knew he was smitten by her, and he was almost unable to tear his gaze away. He bent down to whisper something to one of his men and then gave her one last intense look of longing, and after a brief nod and a smile, he moved on.

Rizpah was visibly shaken by his attention, and that last meaningful stare seemed to convey so much in a split second. She quickly brushed it off as nothing, but it hadn't escaped Huldah's sharp eyes, and she began to tease her friend. They followed behind the crowds and Saul's men for a while and then made their way home. Once there, Rizpah relived every fraction of that encounter in her mind. She just could not believe that she had come so close to Saul and that he had actually noticed her. As she had predicted, the air was full of tales, laughter and jokes about his visit. Everyone had their own account of what they had seen or heard. Rizpah was strangely quiet and had very little to say, and she found herself completely left out of the conversations. Her mind was still racing with thoughts that just could not be shared with anyone, least of all Huldah, who would lose no time in teasing her mercilessly.

Life changes

A few days later, a well-dressed stranger came to Rizpah's house to meet with her parents, and everyone in the area gathered and began to wonder who he was and what business he had with them. He had bodyguards with him, and they had to wait outside too, but they were silent and gave nothing away. After the stranger had left, Rizpah was called into the house. She was told that the man was a servant of King Saul's household. He had come to tell her parents that King Saul wanted her to join his harem as one of his concubines. Having seen her in the crowds, he had instructed his men to find her because he just had to have her.

Rizpah was shocked beyond belief that she had been singled out in this manner. She had always imagined being married to someone local and raising a large family nearby. Now she was being told that she would have to leave the village that had always been her home and must move into the palace. Worse still, she would not even be a respected wife but a sexual plaything based on the whim of the king. Saul commanded her presence because as the king, he could do so, and no one could refuse him. He could also use and discard her like yesterday's newspaper, and no one could do anything about that either.

The servant had told her parents that she should feel honoured and proud to be chosen to serve her king. Rizpah was also wise enough to know that given the social standing of her family, this was a royal command and they would not be in a position to refuse. If they did, the whole family could be put to death; or, if such an extreme measure wasn't taken, their lives could be made very unbearable. Because she was a woman, her fate would depend on her parents. She would have no choice in the matter, irrespective of who had asked for her hand in marriage. The servant told her parents that he would come back the next day at noon. He expected Rizpah to be ready to be collected and transported to the palace.

A new life with the king

The next day Rizpah said a tearful farewell to her parents and her friends and left with the servants to the palace. Once she got there, she was grateful to realise that there would be a grace period before she had to come face to face with the king. This would give her time to sort out the range of conflicting emotions that raced back and forth in her heart and mind. She was angry on the one hand at being selected like a pawn in a chess game over which she had no control or choices. She was also desperately afraid of being away from home in a strange environment with her future uncertain and with no allies to confide in. Rizpah also had an innate sense of desperation and insecurity about what lay ahead. She already missed her family and friends so much. She felt the tears well up in her eyes at the very thought of them. She imagined what each one of them would be doing right now. She longed to be able to hear them laughing and joking or even just telling her it was going to be alright for her.

Yet despite her anger and fear, Rizpah was anxious and excited all at once. She was in a privileged position and she knew it. She remembered how handsome Saul was and how mesmerised she had been by him. Yet she was afraid and worried that she would be found wanting as a woman and would not be able to please him. She was inexperienced, but

Just Want to be Loved for Me...

deep down she hoped that she would learn how to please him and thus find favour with him.

Her only hope of survival would be to learn her trade well and become an expert in how to please the king. This would ensure that his favour would always be with her. Her period of preparation and training would be different to that of a future princess or queen. She would never need to know the etiquette of official court behaviour, or how to raise royal children, or how to run the palace household.

She was taught how to prepare herself for the king through the beauty rituals of bathing, dressing, being perfumed, having perfectly coiffed hair and applying dark eye makeup to give her an alluring appearance. She was also taught how to dance seductively to the beat of the music and to please him sensually. She would learn strategies like how to make just enough eye contact with him to convey the promise of things to come, yet at the same time to know just how to lower her gaze and to peep at him through lowered lashes that fluttered just above the veil she wore on her lower face. This added to the whole process of seduction and resulted in a complex mix of sexual promise combined with mystery. This was designed to ensure that the imagination of the man would go into overdrive. At the end of her training, she would be shown how to follow through and use her body to tantalise, arouse and sexually heighten his pleasure. Now, at last, she was ready to be presented to the king.

Rizpah was a quick study and won favour with Saul immediately. She became one of his favourite bedtime companions. All too soon, though, she found herself pregnant and bore him a son called Armoni. Once a respectable amount of time had passed, Saul sought her out again and she soon bore him another son called Mephibosheth.

Rizpah settles into motherhood

Life settles down for Rizpah now that she has the children to care for. Saul was requesting her presence less and less frequently now, anyway. He was much more taken up with the battles he had to fight, but also with each new concubine that he managed to procure. Rizpah had expected this, and so it came as no surprise to her. It was a woman's lot and that was all there was to it. She had a comfortable life, and she and the children had everything they needed. The situation had worked out well for everyone including her parents and her extended family, who had also benefited from her relationship with the king.

Rizpah's main goal in life was to be the best mother she could be and to make sure that her children were able to learn all that they would need to know to become successful adults. She proudly watched them grow and took pride in everything they achieved. She was especially careful to make sure that they excelled in skills that would put them on a par with the legitimate sons of the king. She could not bear the thought that people might think less of her precious sons because she was 'only' a concubine. After all, it was not their fault, or hers either for that matter.

There might however still be a slight chance of redemption for her sons: If Saul died and there was no legitimate son to take over the throne, it could then be passed on to the illegitimate son who was next in line to inherit. This was very unlikely, but it could happen. If it did, the mother of that son would then become elevated to the

Just Want to be Loved for Me...

top position in the royal household. For this reason, there were many unexplained deaths in the various royal courts. People would vie for position and would oftentimes plot, poison or kill to elevate their positions. This made the job of the king's food tasters more onerous. An assassin would have to be careful to find cunning ways to get past them to inflict their poison or to defeat the highly trained guards who protected the king.

The future looked bright for Rizpah and her sons no matter what might happen. She thought fondly about the nights of passion she had shared with the king, but those were a distant memory now, and her rare meetings with him were mostly about the children. He clearly loved and adored them, too, but he was a busy man with many heavy burdens on his shoulders and was unable to spend that much time with them.

In any event, she was conscious of the steady stream of younger and more beautiful girls arriving at the harem from all over the land. They too had been chosen to serve as concubines and thus needed to be groomed and trained for the role. She watched as each of the young, fresh-faced girls arrived with the same fears she had all those years ago. Each girl secretly harboured the hope that maybe she would be the one to steal the king's heart so that he could never refuse her anything. Dreaming that one day they may be chosen to become his queen, they too would end up disappointed just like all the others. They would also have to find something else to focus on and to immerse themselves in. Ultimately, they too would need to find a dedicated purpose for their lives that did not include King Saul.

There is no way that Rizpah and the other older women could compete with the steady stream of fresh nubile young women who were brought into the harem. This was a world where maturity and experience were not valued. It was all about being young, fresh and beautiful with the sexy curves that would drive the king to distraction. As time went by, Rizpah noticed that the girls seemed to be younger and younger, oftentimes barely verging on the brink between childhood and adulthood. Some of the older women were resentful of them. They treated them badly, often reducing them to tears. Others, like Rizpah, were as helpful as they could be. As an older woman (and thus almost like a motherly figure), she often gave them advice and support, and comforted them as they sobbed into their pillows at night when everyone was asleep. They missed their homes and families and were not always able to cope in this new, often hostile environment.

As Rizpah grew older, she struggled to quell the pangs of loneliness and to banish any thought she had about wanting to be sexy and desirable again. She had to face the harsh reality that there would never be opportunities for her to feel the warmth of a man's embrace again. It was a known fact that once a woman belonged to the king, no one else could have her even after the king had finished with her. This was especially true if she bore him children. Again, this was a woman's lot in life if she had been chosen to join his harem. A mother was not supposed to have sexual feelings or needs, and the closest Rizpah ever got to sex these days was to talk and joke with the other women in the harem about how much they missed those days of anticipation and nights filled with passion.

So Rizpah chose instead to focus on her children; after all, they were all she really had. Even though they were growing up and needing her less with every passing day, she immersed herself in their lives and the exuberant happiness that young people naturally bring into the home. She supported her children in every way that she could and protected them against all harm or danger. So deep was her love and devotion to them, that she would have gladly given her life for them if she had to. After all, her life was technically over now, and she had served her purpose. The future belonged to them. She never could have known that this love and devotion for her children would actually be put to the test, and sooner than she realised.

The death of a king

The day that Rizpah had often feared came, and along with it came the news that Saul had been killed in battle along with Jonathan, his son. As people became aware of the ramifications of this tragic event, a great sense of panic and uncertainty began to sweep the nation. Saul had been their first king, and the people could not imagine what life would be like without him. The next in line to the throne was Jonathan, his eldest son, but he had been killed alongside his father.

Ish-Bosheth, the second son, became king, and this appeased the people slightly and brought a little stability to the throne. However, those who knew him well were very much aware that he was a particularly weak man and would never make a good leader. Abner, the general of the army, was a very cunning and strong leader. He became Ish-Bosheth's close advisor and confidante. The new king was nothing more than a figurehead. The real power lay in

Abner's hands, and he enjoyed this position very much. He was the one who managed the court affairs and had control over all the king's assets.

Soon people began to realise that it was more important to get Abner on their side if they wanted something done. They knew that if he recommended something, King Ish-Bosheth would go along with it. The king was easygoing, gullible and easily influenced. He was not confident or strong enough to make a fuss even if he did not agree with Abner's decisions.

Abner became too confident in his position, and one fine day he took things a little too far. Unknown to Rizpah, he had been watching her for some time now. He had noticed that she was still as beautiful as ever, and the passing years had enhanced her good looks, not faded them. She had also continued to take exceptional care of her body and was as fit as ever. He had often seen her around the palace grounds with her boys and had admired the way she cared for and indulged them. She was still a good catch, and with King Saul out of the way, he decided to claim her as his own concubine. This would solidify his position and authority around the palace. She too would gain importance attached to a powerful man like Abner.

Rizpah, for her part, had never liked Abner; she had always found him too self-assured and sly. Having only ever been intimate with the king, she panicked at the thought of having to answer to another man and having to struggle to please his every wish. She liked her uncomplicated life as it was. Despite the loneliness, she pretty much ran things herself. Abner treated her exactly as Saul had done, in that he did not solicit her own views or willingness. As a woman,

Just Want to be Loved for Me...

things had definitely not changed for her, and she was nothing more than a sexual toy or plaything at the mercy of any man who chose to use her.

Rizpah was older now, and experience had taught her that as a 'toy' she could be played with and discarded at any time. She would never be valued for who she was or what her opinions were. The only skills that mattered now were the ones she had learned all those years ago in preparation to meet Saul. This was the long forgotten art of seduction and pleasure giving. Rizpah was mortified at the very thought of it all and was not willing to play that game all over again. After so many years of inactivity, she had also lost her confidence, and she was under no illusion that a relationship with Abner would be all about sex and nothing more. She was too old and tired to be placed in a situation where she would have to use her body to win sexual favours.

She could not imagine actually being touched by another man, although she had often fantasised about it. She blushed at the very thought that Abner would see her naked and want to be joined intimately with her. Rizpah bowed her head and sighed inwardly, her heart heavy with anxiety. Then, she scolded herself inwardly: she had spent too much time worrying about it already. After all, no one cared about her opinion or the fact that she was still mourning the loss of Saul. Nonetheless, she would have to do whatever she was told irrespective of her feelings on the matter.

Things took an unexpected turn for her. When King Ish-bosheth found out about Abner's plan, he was furious. He took it as a personal insult against the memory of his father that Abner should want to be with Saul's concubine and the mother of his children. Abner had gone too far this time, and Ish-bosheth found his backbone: he made it very clear that it was unacceptable for Abner to take such a personal liberty against the family.

It was highly unusual for Ish-bosheth to take such a stand, as he almost never contradicted anything that Abner said or did. They fell out about it and this led to Abner switching his loyalties away from this weak king. He made a deal with David to help him overthrow Ish-bosheth and unite the people under a single ruler. This plan worked really well and David became the overall king. However, there was more trouble in store for Abner under this new arrangement. Joab, the general of David's army, disliked Abner intensely and viewed him as a threat to his own position. He was also unhappy about the two nations being joined together, especially because it was the result of Abner's plan. He plotted against Abner and ultimately killed him. This finally left Rizpah free to continue her life as before without Abner's impending threat looming over her.

Famine in the land

Under David's united rule, there was a big problem to contend with and that was the issue of widespread famine in the land. After three years of having used every strategy they could think of to solve the problem, it was time for a different approach. David decided that it was time to ask God for the reason and to implore him to intervene in the situation.

David is told that the famine is the result of a judgement on the people because of Saul's past actions. Saul had previously negotiated a treaty with the Gibeonites. He had later gone directly against it and tried to commit genocide

Just Want to be Loved for Me...

on their people. This violated the treaty, which reflected negatively on the integrity of his word and his leadership qualities.

In an effort to resolve this problem, David apologised to the survivors of the Gibeonites and offered payment to make amends. They immediately refused the payment and instead, demanded the ultimate price. That is, they wanted nothing less than 'an eye for an eye and a tooth for a tooth' – but in this case, it was more like blood for blood. David was given no choice, and therefore he chose seven of Saul's surviving relatives to be offered up to the Gibeonites as reparation. He chose five of Saul's grandsons through his daughter Merab and both of Rizpah's sons.

Judgement for Saul's family

It all happened so quickly and without warning or even explanation. Early one morning as the family were having breakfast, men from David's army appeared at the house. Rizpah's two sons were seized, handcuffed and led away. She watched, horrified and unable to make sense of what was going on. Her screams for the men to stop were lost in the din of confusion as people came from everywhere to see what was going on. The soldiers were under strict instructions to remove the boys and not to engage with the people on the matter. There was anger and frustration as the local men tried to reason with them, and the sound of wailing as the women helplessly stood by confused, unable to comprehend what wrong the young men had committed.

Rizpah and some of the others followed them, and their anguish increased when they realised why the boys had been taken. They watched, horrified, as the seven innocent young men were all handed over to the Gibeonites to satisfy their need for revenge against the boys' father and grandfather, Saul.

What bitter irony for this to happen in April in the midst of glorious springtime when new life was in abundance everywhere. New blossoms were peeping out shyly from their opening buds. New crops were shooting up from the rich soil and beginning their climb towards the warmth of the sun. Newly born animals filled the barns. Spring is a time of new life, yet this was the time chosen for Rizpah's sons to die the most horrific death for a sin they did not commit.

Rizpah had not slept a full night since the day they were taken. Her eyes were red and swollen from crying, her shoulders were stooped in despair, and her body was aching all over from the anguish and pain that racked and ravaged her whole being. She experienced every possible emotion in quick succession, one after another. She was angry at everything and everyone. She was hurt with the unbelievable pain of a mother's sorrow. Her babies needed her and this time she was not able to be there for them. This was something she could not fix or make better. She could not bear to be apart from them and yet she could not bear to stand idly by and just watch as their fate unfolded. She desperately prayed as she had never prayed before, willing a miracle to happen so that her sons' fate could be reversed.

The miracle she prayed for did not come to pass, however. After much deliberation, she chose to witness their execution on a mountaintop near Saul's homeland. Even if she could not help them, she would at least be there as they drew their last breath. It was the only thing left for her to do for her

Just Want to be Loved for Me...

sons – the final act of motherly love she could show them. They knew that she was there, and she noticed that they had already been beaten and tortured beforehand. She saw the pain and anguish in their eyes along with the bewilderment of not quite being able to understand how this had happened to them.

Each of her sons died a slow and painful death after being impaled on a stake. Each agonising scream tore into Rizpah's heart, searing it like a hot iron. It was more than she could bear, but she needed to be there for them until the end. She prayed that God would grant them a merciful and swift release from their pain and sorrows. Eventually it was all over and she heard the last whimper of pain and the last rasping breath. Then there was a heavy silence and an eerie stillness as death hung in the air like a cloud over the mountaintop. People slowly began to wander away, satisfied that their revenge was now complete. The bodies were left there, open and exposed to the elements as an example to all.

The aftermath

Rizpah slowly made her way home, each step more laboured than the last. Unable to shed any more tears, the pain hung in her heart like a lead balloon, weighing her down so that she resembled an old lady hobbling along on her last legs. She asked herself the same questions over and over again. How on earth was she going to face life without her sons? She had nothing left, especially now that Saul was dead too. She had nothing to show for her life, and her future was now very uncertain. Had it really all been for nothing? Her heart and mind were just too full of conflicting thoughts and emotions, with each vying for attention over the others. Her head ached and she stroked her temples in a bid to relieve the pain brought on by the stress of the whole ordeal.

Rizpah had never been a quitter, though. As she pondered her life without her sons, she knew that surely there had to be something she could do to turn her situation around.

It came to her in a flash, and suddenly, she knew what she must do. She collected some sackcloth and took it back to the mountaintop. Once there she lovingly placed it over her children and sat with them. The cloth was symbolic of her state of mourning, and as she sat there holding silent vigil, she took the time to go over things in her mind. She knew that the boys were now in a better place and that death had come as a welcome release for them. Their battered and bruised bodies looked nothing like the vibrant boys she had raised to manhood. She remembered how proud she had been of them when they were born. She had lovingly examined every perfect part of them as she held them secure in her arms. She remembered playing with them and delighting in their squeals of laughter, and she fondly remembered her intermittent frustration with them every time they fought with each other and made up again.

As she sat there quietly beside her sons' bodies, she had nothing but time to allow each memory to unfold at random. She experienced all the emotions of motherhood again as they washed over her in waves. She remembered her joy as her sons took their first steps and spoke their first words. She has been filled with pride at each of their achievements. She had panicked every time they were ill or

Just Want to be Loved for Me...

hurting, and had worried each time they left the house until they had returned safely.

Being a mother was such a blessing, but in her situation, it felt like a curse. One of the hardest things a mother can endure is watching her child die. It causes a depth of pain that is second to none, and just contemplating the loss of a child brings a mother's worst fears to the surface. It somehow feels unnatural, as if the correct order of events has been all mixed up.

Rizpah had always imagined that she would live to an old age and her sons would bury her long before they too died after living a good long life. When the tables were turned on her, it was one of the hardest things to face. She found it almost impossible to walk away from their crude burial place leaving her beloved children behind instead of bringing them back with her in the comfort and safety of her home and arms. She found herself fighting hard to hang on to the fact that their creator had recalled them. She struggled to accept that they were no longer her responsibility and that her work with them was done. There was nothing else she could do. She would have to accept certain truths as the reality of her life now as she struggled to move on and find some meaning in her daily existence.

Rizpah's vigil

As the hours went by and the stiffness of death set into her sons' bodies, scavengers and predatory animals began prowling around, hungry for their next meal. In horror at the thought of animals getting at her sons' bodies, and with the fierceness that only a mother can conjure, Rizpah fought off the vultures that tried to tear at their rotting flesh and pick out their eyes from their sockets. The jackals hung around howling and waiting for an opportunity to rip the flesh off her precious sons' bones. Rizpah summoned the strength to scare them away, her mind barely having time to comprehend the horror of what she was having to do, as if watching her sons being tormented to death hadn't been agony enough.

In this way, the revenge of the Gibeonites continued even in death; her sons were not afforded a decent burial but were left to the mercy of the wild animals and the elements, their only staunch defender being their beloved mother.

Though Rizpah had no say over whether it was right for her sons to be taken and killed, the act of protecting her sons' bodies from the ravenous beasts was at least one thing she could control. She chose to exercise her right to do so and to honour them in death so that their carcasses would not end up being strewn across the land.

Rizpah stayed there for a long time keeping watch over his sons and fighting off the predators. This gave her some time to really mourn the loss of her sons in private. It also gave her the opportunity to look to God to direct her life and to help her find a new purpose for what was left of it.

Her family and friends came to visit her on the mountaintop to encourage her to see sense and to give up her vigil, but she would not be moved. They settled instead for bringing her food and water so that she would be able to survive this period in her life.

As the months went by, Rizpah braved the intense heat of the summer followed by the cold desert conditions

Just Want to be Loved for Me...

of winter on the mountaintop. She was not sure how this would end, but she knew that something had to happen and eventually there would be a breakthrough.

Her prayers brought her closer to God as she communed with him throughout the long weary hours. She prayed for strength to see things through. She also asked for the ability to be able to release the Gibeonites from the mental prison she had created in her mind because of the hate she nursed for them. Rizpah knew that she would never be able to move on with her life without forgiving them. God would never be able to do his work in her with this blockage of hate in her heart, which affected every thought and clouded her every judgement. The hate seemed to have overcome her very being and permeated into the very sinews of her flesh. It had come long after the anger had subsided, and it had replaced the victimisation mode that had followed the anger. It made her feel sorry for herself and her situation. She constantly felt hard done by and frequently asked the question, *Why me?*

The breakthrough came after six long months into her vigil. By now, she had been led into a place of quiet acceptance. She had renewed her relationship with God, and she was now in a place of total surrender. God could fill her empty, broken body with his healing spirit. Her broken will was now in a place where it was pliable enough for God to use her for his own purpose without her own human will creating any obstacles. She was now ready to move on.

King David heard of her vigil and her devotion. His heart was moved with compassion, and so he ordered his soldiers to collect the remains of all the sons on the mountaintop. He also commanded that Saul and Jonathan's bodies be brought home as well. All of them were given a decent burial together. This act marked the end of the drought and the rains finally came, allowing the people to move on with their lives.

Rizpah was now freed from her vigil; at last, her sons would be honoured with a decent resting place beside their father. Her work on the mountaintop was done and she was now free to pick up the shards of her broken life and move forward.

Rizpah's story is a powerful example of a mother's love for her sons. It is also about the need to honour and protect the people you love, even in the face of death. Finally, it is a lesson to us about the importance of honouring your word and preserving your dignity in the face of difficulties by not giving up.

Rizpah's ordeal foreshadows Mary's

In the Bible, we also read of Mary in the New Testament, the most blessed of all women because she was chosen to bring forth the Messiah. This was a big responsibility for an unmarried teen girl, who never would have put herself in such a complex situation to begin with. She chose to obey God and carry the child that the Holy Spirit had placed within her, even though there was a chance that she would be labelled a harlot if Joseph refused to marry her so that the child could be raised in a family setting.

Like Rizpah before her, Mary would also have to face the cruel death of her son, Jesus, which was necessary for the scriptures to be fulfilled and salvation to come to mankind. Mary would experience the same anguish as Rizpah and would witness her innocent son brutally beaten

Just Want to be Loved for Me...

and crucified in front of her. Even though she knew he was born to fulfil a purpose, she still would have suffered the same pain Rizpah had endured in ultimately seeing her son die horribly in this way. The punishment of the cross was reserved for the worst criminals, and Mary must have agonised trying to understand what her son Jesus had done to deserve it. She too, would have been torn in the same way that Rizpah had been. Mary had to decide whether to stay away or be there to witness her son's crucifixion. Like Rizpah, she also chose to be there for her son in his final painful moments, though there was nothing she could do for him in his helpless state.

Fighting off modern-day vultures and jackals

This incredible story of a mother's love is able to transcend time, culture and location. The strength of this love is second to none, and there are so many examples of mothers who place the needs of their children far above their own. If mothers around the world could be asked on any given day to describe the extreme circumstances they have had endure for the sake of their children, there would countless stories of bravery and sacrifices made in order to ensure that the next generation are given the best possible access to all kinds of opportunities and comforts.

It is unlikely that mothers today will ever have to face what Rizpah and Mary endured. However, many mothers do find themselves fighting tirelessly on behalf of their children, particularly their sons, to prevent them from being consumed by the modern equivalents of vultures and jackals that would seek to maim and destroy their precious sons. These come in a variety of forms. Mothers today fight the impact that drugs, alcohol, gang and spiritual warfare, guns, knives, violence, peer pressure, musical and lyrical influences, and rampant sexual immorality have on their sons.

The jackals and vultures are disguised in so many different ways that it takes a spiritually astute woman to recognise them and to deal with them. So many mothers have lost their sons to these things. Sometimes this has even resulted in their sons' death. More often, it results in the inability of their sons to engage with and take their place in society as fully active citizens who make a positive impact. This renders them as social outcasts and disconnects them from all the things they hold dear.

Painfully, this often includes families and local communities. Too many young men find solace in others who are experiencing the same symptoms as themselves. They validate one another's negative feelings and experiences. They are unable to bring a sensible word of hope or offer solutions for finding their way back home, whether literally or figuratively. We live in a transient world where long-term loyalty and commitment are rare. People come and go, and each broken life is affected in different ways.

Modern mothers can take a page out of Rizpah's book. She was driven by her love and devotion to her sons. She chose to stand by them even when things looked as though they couldn't get any worse. Her sacrifice won her favour from King David and her sons got the ultimate resting place that she had wanted for them. In death, they received the honour and respect they were denied in life.

Over the course of my working life, I have met all kinds of mothers from a variety of age ranges and cultures. The

Just Want to be Loved for Me...

Rizpah spirit is alive and well today. I have seen mothers supporting their sons who have committed yet another crime. These women have tried everything in their power to encourage their sons to change their behaviour to no avail. Their devotion is unquestionable as they turn up for court again and again, worn down and tired by the system but still willing to do whatever it takes to redeem their sons. Whether it is to offer their homes as a bail address or to assist in paying off their sons' fines, their support never ceases.

Sometimes mothers find themselves supporting sons that have fallen prey to destructive and addictive behaviour, usually through drink or drugs. Mothers tirelessly support them through the painful rehabilitation process again and again. Others find themselves at a loss as to how to rescue their sons from anti-social behaviour and crimes of violence. Even more heartbreaking are the mothers who stand helplessly by watching their sons greedily profit from selling the drugs that destroy and break the lives of others. The dealers climb the social ladder living a life of luxury, with expensive cars, designer clothes and jewellery. Their manipulation of others allows them to eat at the most exclusive restaurants and party at the trendiest hotspots.

On the other hand, the drug users' lives are immersed with thoughts and plans of how to get their next fix, and they sink deeper and deeper into an abyss of loss and despair. They are constantly scheming for ways to find the money to buy more drugs, and their hunger for them is never satisfied. Loyalties to families and possessions disappear as each one becomes only as valuable as how much money they can be conned out of or sold for to buy the next fix.

Other women find themselves with sons who have chosen to opt out of life completely. They sleep well past midday every day, and then after a shower and change, they meet up with their friends and stay up all night. They spend their time playing computer games, drinking, smoking cannabis and playing around with girls. There is no thought for working, studying or planning for their future. This lethargic and chaotic lifestyle means that they are unable to engage in traditional life patterns. They find themselves unable to become engaged in timetabled study or work, and some are even unable to wake up in time to sign onto the Internet to collect their benefits from the government for not working!

Mothers find themselves at a loss to understand these behaviour patterns. They ask themselves how this could have happened, and they are completely unable to relate to this way of life. This is especially true if they have brought up their children to have honesty, integrity and due regard for the law. These mothers struggle to understand where things went wrong because they know they instilled core moral values in their sons in terms of ambition, work and planning for their future.

Then there are the mothers whose perfect little sons grow up and reject the family and their upbringing completely. They feel that the core values they have learned are somehow backward and not something they can identify with now. These sons seldom if ever visit the family and seem to care very little about whether they are coping. They are unwilling to assist their families financially, emotionally or physically. They may even have adopted other people whom they are more willing to treat as family. In selfishness, they opt to leave the full financial burden on the rest of the family. The

Just Want to be Loved for Me...

mothers of these uncaring sons question their behaviour and rearing methods over and over again, searching to find an explanation of why their sons have done this to them, wondering where they went wrong.

Moving on

Whatever the story, when a mother is hurt by her son(s), it puts her in such a painful situation that she desperately seeks to find solutions. No matter how old their sons get, most mothers feel a heavy responsibility toward them. Once again, we need to learn from Rizpah's example.

Like Rizpah, women need to reach out to the Almighty God for his direction and guidance in difficult times. Rizpah stopped looking inward for the answers and began looking upward. She did the only thing left within her power, and that was to pray. We all know that prayer does indeed change things. God hears all prayers, and he is often moved to compassion by fervent requests. He can use a bad situation to turn things around for everyone. The son's life may be changed for the better, and quite often, he will find a new relationship with God as well. A mother's relationship with God may reach a new level as she spends more time with him in prayer and reading his Word. She will begin to understand him better as she surrenders more of herself to God, thus allowing him to work in her life as well.

By the time David decreed that Rizpah's sons were to be given a proper burial, she had already been alone with God for a long time. She had spent much time talking to him, praying, and praising him, and sometimes she had just sat quietly listening to his voice. He had brought her to a place of peace and security at the end. She was so desperate for something to happen that she may not have realised that he was holding her hand throughout one of the most difficult situations she would ever have to face in her entire life. It would tear at the very fibre of her being and challenge every preconceived thought she may have had. Yet in the darkness of her bereavement, when she thought she was alone, God was there.

God is the same today as he was then; you can know for certain that he is there with you in your situation. Whatever it may be, you need to know that you have the solution right there within you. All you have to do is to reach out with all your heart, surrender and allow his will to become your own. Then you will see the breakthrough happen. This process is a journey that will allow you to develop into who God wants you to be. It is often through difficulties that we find not only ourselves but also God, and we find out who we are *in* God. So don't lose heart if it doesn't happen all at once.

Have hope, take heart and finally, let God take over. Let him lead you and your sons into the life he has planned for you from the very beginning. Then you will at last truly know and experience ***his*** peace in your life.

Chapter Seven

Sensuality: Blessing or Curse?

Delilah's Story

Introduction

In this chapter, I want to talk to you about the allure of a woman's sexuality. As the title suggests, there is a lot riding on the nature of her choices, as well as how she may elect to use her sensuality. In some circumstances, it may be that her choices lead her to become a blessing to a man. Sadly, in other scenarios, her choice may decidedly become a curse, either for herself or for the man to whom her sensuality is directed, as well as a curse to other people in that man's life who will experience the repercussions of her behaviour.

In many ways, it may help to start right at the very beginning and examine the multi faceted functions that women have. Women are able to attend to many different tasks simultaneously and to work their way systematically through the complexities of modern life relatively easily. This innate feminine skill has been learnt and passed down through the ages. In fact, it is this suggestion of ease that creates many problems in itself. The role of women has been undermined and undervalued since the beginning of recorded human history. Women are seen as 'just' housewives or homemakers. There is no recognition for the plethora of tasks women accomplish with ease or our ability to juggle many different roles and responsibilities at the same time.

In my first job as Project Manager for a new programme, my boss instructed me to handle the tasks in the same way I would do if I were moving into a new home. This meant that in setting up the project, I had to ensure that the utilities were all supplied. I had to negotiate with the builders who were refurbishing the property to ensure they completed their work on time. After this, the next stage was to do with decorating and furnishing. This largely meant that I had to ensure that all the equipment was bought and supplied cost-effectively. This ranged from choosing the flooring right down to making sure that there were paper clips available to keep papers together. This called for a methodical approach and an eye for detail.

This advice from my new boss proved to be one of the best pieces of advice I could have been given to accomplish the multitude of tasks involved. As a wife and mother, I had done these tasks for my home many times. I had also become adept at strategic planning for the household to include strict financial accounting, as well as monitoring and evaluation skills in assessing how well things were running. On a practical level, I had to ensure that the shopping, cooking, cleaning and childcare were provided for. I did all of this in addition to working full time and volunteering in my church community. As a modern woman, I am not alone in having to multi task my way through life; many women find themselves having to cope with similar situations.

The other aspect of a woman's life has to do with her sexuality, and sometimes it can be challenging to know how this should manifest itself in modern life. The first thing to acknowledge is that this is almost a taboo subject.

Women are not encouraged to talk openly about or even to display any hint of sexuality or prowess. This is because they are aware of this unspoken societal rule, the women who *do* express their sensuality live with an undercurrent of guilt. There is a feeling of frustration or inadequacy when they are not able to follow the 'respectable' mode of behaviour. These women are generally not valued and are regarded as cheap. They are seen as good to look at and even to liaise with, but are rarely taken seriously enough to marry.

Just Want to be Loved for Me...

Young women are often shown examples of women they should avoid being like at all costs. Secretly many women admire these women who are comfortable with their sensuality; they find them attractive, and they long to be like them. Most women, however, will ultimately give in to the pressure to conform to the societal rules. They too will deny the sensual side of themselves in order to fit in.

This is especially true in Christian circles, where women are respected for looking and dressing a certain way. It is quite often unheard of for Christian women to be holy and sexy in the same body. As a result, they often appear dull and unattractive. Many people take the scripture in 1 Peter 2:9 literally, which says that Christians should be a 'peculiar people'. This justifies the thinking of others who consider them weird and strange. This often isolates young women who would love to worship God but are reluctant to surrender their lives to a dull and seemingly boring life where people will just look at them with pity and think they are weird.

Sexuality is a perfectly natural feminine attribute and can be used to wield great power and influence over the male members of our species. We find ourselves asking if the Bible has anything to say on the matter. I was most surprised to find through my research that my own views were challenged.

The woman I want to talk about in this section was named Delilah. You can read her story in the Book of Judges chapter 16 from verse 4 onwards. Her story is a well-known one and has been made the subject of many films and documentaries. All of them seem to portray her in a similar way, and it is mostly from a negative perspective. She is portrayed as a sexually astute individual, and her profile is so bad that little girls are never named after her.

In modern times, the popularity of Biblical names goes in a cyclical trend, which has given rise to lots of baby girls named Hannah, Elizabeth, Esther, Ruth, Naomi and Deborah to name a few, but Delilah has never been a trendy name because it is associated with negative images of sexual manipulation and deceit. So let us now see what we can find out about the lady herself.

The story begins

Delilah was born in the valley of Sorek, which is about twenty kilometres southwest of Jerusalem. In Hebrew Sorek means 'vineyard valley'. This piece of land was occupied by the Philistines at the time.

It might help to put Delilah's story into perspective if I tell you that this story takes place after the Hebrew people have been delivered from Egypt through the leadership of Moses. They had been in the bondage of slavery for about four hundred years. Then, after the exodus, they spent forty years wandering aimlessly in the wilderness looking for the Promised Land. An entire generation had passed during this time.

At the time when Delilah's story takes place, the Hebrew people are now living in Canaan, the Promised Land, under the leadership of Joshua. They had conquered and claimed the land from the existing people as they moved inland. This was in direct accordance with the promise that God had given to Abraham about his descendants.

Just Want to be Loved for Me...

Very early on, the Hebrews came into contact with the Philistines, who were also strangers in the land. The Philistines were known as the 'Sea People', and history records that they invaded both Egypt and Canaan around 1000 BC. They were a strong people and were known to have large well-disciplined armies. They were also more advanced in terms of technology and had superior iron weapons. In Egypt, they were driven off by Ramses before they could take a foothold. However, in Canaan, they managed to get in with less resistance and they built five large city-states. Each of the states was ruled by a Philistine ruler who was able to exert a lot of power locally and had full control of the armies in the area.

Prior to coming into Canaan, the Hebrew people were used to moving around a lot, and now they struggled to settle down in this new land and stake out areas that they could call their own. This caused them to have much conflict with the Philistines, who were also trying to hang on to and expand their authority in the same areas. The Hebrew people were suffering under their strict governance and they cried out to God for help. There was much enmity and fighting between their people. This had gone on for about forty years now, and the time was ripe for God to act and to send them a deliverer.

Delilah

As I said earlier, we know very little about Delilah. Furthermore, there is no confirmation in the Bible as to whether she was Philistine or Hebrew. Interestingly enough, there is no consensus about what her name even means. Some say that in Hebrew her name means 'delicate or dainty one', and others say it means 'night or dark'. In Arabic it means 'flirtatious or coquettish woman', but whether this meaning was attached to it after her dalliance with Samson is not known. In many ways, if she were a Hebrew woman, the original storytellers would have been quick to distance themselves from her because of the negative impact she had on their lives.

Almost nothing is known about her early life, and the first we hear of her is when she is approached by the five Philistine rulers. We do know that she had her own home, which is where she spent time with Samson. If we look at this situation a little closer, we will find that she was probably a widow or a prostitute. Women at that time in history were either their fathers' property before they were married or their husbands' property afterwards. They had very little rights and would probably not even be able to own land in their own names. So something had to have happened in Delilah's life that enabled her to live alone in her own home.

Whether she was a Hebrew or a Philistine, the important thing to emphasise here is that she was a woman in a world dominated by men where women were seldom able to wield any power. I use the word seldom here because I am reminded of the story of another strong woman in the Old Testament, a woman called Deborah, who was one of the judges. For all intents and purposes, she is portrayed in the Bible as a businesswoman, but she was also very highly regarded as a leader. She was raised up by God to advise and lead the people. She instructed Barak to lead the army in battle. So great was her authority, that Barak was only able to lead that army with confidence if she accompanied him.

Just Want to be Loved for Me...

This she did and a great victory was achieved. You can read her story in the book of Judges chapter 4.

Samson

When we take a closer look at the story of Delilah, the Bible tells us that she was loved by Samson. It may help a little if we understand the man that Samson was, and why such a liaison between him and Delilah was so important during the time in which they lived.

Samson was born for a specific purpose, and he was a special gift to both his family and his people. Up until he was conceived, his parents had not been able to have children. Manoah and his wife, who were from the tribe of Dan, were chosen by God to raise Samson. They were given very strict instructions about who he was and how he was to be raised. They were told that he would be a Nazirite. This meant that he would be consecrated to God from birth. As a Nazirite he should never drink wine or strong drink, and he should remain unshaven always. Samson would eventually become one of the judges who would provide leadership and for his people, and he would also become their champion.

Delilah had heard about Samson long before she met him. People around her talked about him all the time. She heard about his many exploits in battle. He was a one-man army and people were afraid of him. I very much get the image of the actor Sylvester Stallone, and the character he plays in the Rambo movies. Rambo is only one man fighting against an army, but he strategically and methodically takes people out and seems to be unbeatable. He will only be captured when he allows himself to be. Samson was this kind of man. He was unbeatable in battle, something that no one had ever seen before. His exploits were famous, and he was a living legend.

Delilah had also heard about Samson's physical attributes. Besides his superhuman strength, he was known for being tall and strikingly handsome. She knew he had an eye for the ladies, and they flocked around him endlessly. They crooned over him and made themselves readily available to him. They were all drawn by his sheer physical strength and his powerful looking stature. They would all give anything to have this man under their spell.

Delilah was no different and she listened to the stories with great interest. Despite the heroism that everyone revered, she noticed that he also presented himself as a bad boy rebel. She knew that he had already been married once, and that had ended in disaster. This did not surprise her in the least. Samson was a Hebrew, and from all the accounts she had heard, he had been born as a special gift to his people. They viewed him as a saviour and he was highly esteemed. Yet he had chosen to marry a Philistine woman instead of a Hebrew. This meant he had chosen to operate outside the will of his family and his God.

Delilah could not understand how he had been allowed to do this. The Philistines were his enemies. She knew that the Hebrew women were all disappointed that their hero had chosen to marry outside their people. This put paid to every Hebrew mother's hope that her daughter might grow up to become Samson's bride and continue his line and legacy. As for the Philistines, they greeted the news with shock and anger. It was bad enough that Samson regularly defeated their men in battle, but now he had married one of their women. The whole scenario was a non-starter from the

Just Want to be Loved for Me...

beginning. His Philistine wife, who was a pagan worshipper of the god 'Dagon', would be unevenly yoked to him, and therefore she would not share his vision of the calling that God had placed on his life. This would be contrary to the will of God. When God intended man to have a wife as a 'helpmeet', he did so to enable the man to have someone who could 'meet' him in his vision to help him take it forward and achieve it.

Nonetheless, the marriage of Samson and the Philistine woman commences. After the wedding ceremony is over and the celebrations are taking place, Samson poses a riddle for his guests with the promise of garments and other special items of clothing to be given to the winner. If no one can guess the riddle, then the clothing will go to him instead.

Samson's wife comes under intense pressure from her people to get the answer from him so that she can tell it to them. When she hesitates, they accuse her of selling out and wanting to help her husband so that the two of them can keep the prizes for themselves. Her loyalty comes up for question, and so she gives in and begins to persuade Samson to give her the answer. Samson has a weakness for women and cannot bear his new bride's constant nagging for the answer to the riddle, and so he tells her.

Modern men

This reminds me of many men today who are the very image and likeness of Samson, the strong alpha male. They are strong in leadership, battle, resilience and endeavour. Yet these very men can be reduced to an emotional heap when it comes to affairs of the heart. No matter how tough they are, a certain woman is able to come along and infiltrate the finer elements of a man's toughest resolve. She is able to manipulate a situation to her way of thinking, and he is powerless to do anything about it. His sense of right and wrong, fair play, justice or practicality goes totally out of the window. This is the very allure and power of a woman's sensuality.

As a child, I remember vividly hearing people rave on and on about a classic song by Percy Sledge called "When a Man Loves a Woman". He sings about how a man will give all his comforts and sleep out in the rain or even turn his back on his best friend if that friend speaks out against the woman he loves. This song was so popular and successful because its words are so true. Many men, including famous ones have been built up or brought down by the very women they love. When a man is completely captivated by a woman, he is unable to heed any warning about what her real motives may be; all he knows is how wonderful she makes him feel when he is with her.

Samson's rage

Thinking back on Samson's wedding and the whole mess about the riddle, Delilah still remembers the huge commotion that ensued in the local area after Samson told his wife the answer to the riddle. Of course, she had promptly told her people the answer and they had claimed the prize. Samson was so angry when he learned he had been duped that he went down to Ashkelon and killed thirty innocent men there, and then he took their garments and gave them to the people who had answered the riddle.

In his anger, he forgot to return home to his wife but went back to his father's house instead. Samson was soon to

Just Want to be Loved for Me...

get even angrier and out of control. After he cooled down he went back to see his wife, only to discover that her father had given her in marriage to the man who had been the best man at their wedding. Not only had Samson lost the bet for the riddle, but he had also now lost his wife and been betrayed by her father and by his best man, who was also Samson's friend.

Samson burned uncontrollably with rage; he felt so hard done by. He caught three hundred foxes and paired them together tail by tail. Afterwards he torched the tails and set them all free. The animals fled into the fields and this caused all the grains, vineyards and olive groves to be burned to the ground. When the Philistines found out that Samson had done this, they retaliated by burning his former wife and her father. Samson swore vengeance against them for this and went to the rock at Etam. His own people came to him and were very angry with him. They were afraid that the Philistines would take action on them. After all, they were the strongest rulers in the area. Samson allowed them to take him prisoner but made them promise that they would not kill him themselves, but that they would hand him over to the Philistines.

When they arrived and the Philistines descended upon them, the spirit of the Lord came upon Samson even though he was bound, and he was strengthened. He broke free and killed a thousand men with a donkey's jawbone that he found lying on the ground nearby. God gave him the strength to defeat the enemy. When he cried out for thirst, God split open a rock and water poured out from it. This water revived him and he was able to go on to fulfil his purpose – that of being a judge for his people.

Delilah was very observant, however; she noted that Samson still did not stay true to his calling after this. The Bible records yet another instance of him going down to Gaza to a harlot's house. Once the local people knew he was there, they sought to surround the house to kill him.

Delilah knew about all of this and yet she felt an undeniable fascination toward him, despite the fact that he didn't seem to be loyal to his people, his God or his calling. She was excited by how dangerous he was and the fact that he seemed to be a bit of a loose cannon. As a woman with no real rights, she liked the way he stood up to the Philistine rulers. She too saw him as a hero. There was no way that she or most of the other local people could ever stand up to the authorities and have them on the run. She knew that they were worried about him and were always on the lookout for ways they could capture him and somehow weaken him.

They meet at last

Although she had always secretly hoped that she might meet Samson one day, nothing prepared her for the day when that actually happened. She was on her way back from the market where she had been collecting her weekly supplies. As she neared her home, she noticed a large number of men standing around on the street corner, and there was much laughter and bantering going on. They were being positively loud and were jovially facing off at each other, testing their strength and comparing their weapons. She easily recognised a few of the men as her neighbours. As she walked past, they paused to say hello to her.

One man stood out from the crowd, a man who was a stranger to these parts. He was taller and more robustly built

Just Want to be Loved for Me...

than the others were. His powerful stature carried a presence and commanded a level of authority that was consistent with a senior officer in the army, yet he was not dressed as one of them. He was dressed in expensive cloth with a simple yet elegant style. His large head boasted a full beard, a strong hard jaw line and full lips. He had a wild aura about him, which was accentuated by his long unruly hair with its dark, bouncy curls straining against the string he had used to tie them back with careless abandon.

He oozed masculinity and sensuality, and when he smiled at Delilah his large dark eyes seemed to pull her in. She blushed at once, and after a brief smile in his direction, she quickly moved on. She later found out that this handsome stranger was indeed the famous Samson she had heard so much about. She went over the encounter again and again in her mind. She had so many questions, and yet she was afraid to ask anyone for fear that she would give them the wrong impression of the reason for her interest. She wondered what he was doing in this area or who he had come to see.

Her interest in him was growing by the minute. She wondered if she would see him again, and she berated herself for not making more of the brief encounter she'd had with him, which had been a mere glance, but oh, what a glance. He was more handsome and attractive than any of the stories she had heard about him had led her to believe. They simply had not done him justice. She could immediately see why so many women would give anything to have his attention. One thing was sure: if she ever came across him again, she would be ready for the encounter, and she would do everything in her power to make it count.

Luckily for her, she did not have to wait too long. She found out that Samson too had been deeply attracted to her and had also been asking many questions about her. One day he just seemed to turn up as she was sitting and talking to some of the other women in the area. Thankfully, it was on a day that she had worn her best shawl and had taken care with her makeup. She was a beauty and was much sought after by the local men, but sometimes familiarity breeds contempt, and she knew far too much about the men in her village to ever want to be with any of them anyway. She knew that she would never give any of them a chance to win her favour. She would only ever give her heart to someone from outside her local area. Even then, she was cautious. As a single woman, she had already faced much hardship, and her future was not as secure as she would have liked. Yet she knew that if she married the wrong person, he could make her life a misery if he chose to, and she would be powerless to do anything about it.

The relationship blossoms

Samson seemed to be different from any other man she had ever met before. She was amazed to find that beneath that tough exterior beat the heart of a very gentle person. She found him easy to talk to, and they spent many hours enjoying each other's company and talking about all sorts of things. He was sensitive and had a good sense of right and wrong. He was committed to his people but sometimes buckled under the pressure of the many responsibilities placed upon him. It was at these times that he rebelled and walked out of his destiny.

Delilah got a good sense of the God he and his people revered so much. She found out that although his God

Just Want to be Loved for Me...

was invisible, he operated with such love, mercy and grace. She somehow understood that it was the grace and mercy of his God that kept him safe each time he strayed away from his destiny and that always gave him victory over his enemies. Samson told her stories of his people and their history. Delilah was reminded of how the great forefathers Abraham, Isaac and Jacob had walked with God, and how they had been used to bless their people.

Delilah was reminded of the events surrounding his special birth and the purpose he would be called to fulfil. She also understood how sacred his role as a Nazirite was. It was easy to see that he was truly a champion of the people. He had the strength of several men coupled with the wisdom and sensitivity he needed to be a good leader for his people.

By the time the relationship between them became a physical one, they were already well bonded emotionally. Delilah had already let go of many of her doubts and fears that she'd originally had concerning Samson and concerning her life in general. For the first time in a very long time, the future seemed bright to her. Her confidence and self-esteem grew under the covering of this powerful and strong man. Her fears of being married to a man who would make her life intolerable diminished by the minute.

She relished having Samson's love and support. She was constantly amazed at how a man so mighty in battle and strength could be so meek and vulnerable in her arms, sometimes needing her so much that it went to the point of distraction, yet he was as gentle as a lamb when he lovingly caressed her. She loved nothing more than to feel his powerful arms surrounding and comforting her.

Delilah would often throw her arms around his neck, pressing herself against his long hard body. She would gently stroke and run her fingers through his thick curly hair. She became lost in the intensity of love in his eyes as he gazed down at her entranced and planted feather-light kisses on her face and hair. When they were passionately joined together as one flesh, their world became one and nothing else mattered. They were invincible and no one could come between them.

Samson's relationship with Delilah was destined to be a very important episode in his life; as the Bible tells us in Judges 16 verse 4, he 'loved a woman…whose name was Delilah'. This was therefore not a casual relationship, and the word 'loved' is only used in relation to Delilah. When I first read this, I was uplifted to realise that after all he had been through, after all the disappointments and casual dalliances he appeared to have had, he had finally found love. This would have been a good place to end the story except that life is never as neat and tidy as we expect it to be.

The Philistines take action

Samson's past is about to catch up with him. The things he committed while he was on a vengeful angry spree had not been forgotten. The Philistines and his other enemies were always on the lookout for what he is up to, and they were not going to miss an opportunity to exact their revenge on him.

The five Philistine rulers decide to meet to discuss the important matters at hand, and they discover that Samson

Just Want to be Loved for Me...

has settled into a relationship with Delilah. They decide to use this situation to accomplish their own purposes. They are aware from his previous actions that he has a particular weakness when it comes to dealing with females.

All five of the rulers go to see Delilah in a bid to enlist her help in discovering Samson's weaknesses, and to help them determine how best to capture him.

You can imagine how frightening it must have been for Delilah to receive a visit from the five most powerful men in the region. She is just a simple woman who goes about her average daily life (other than the fact that she loves Samson), and she cannot imagine what business they could have with her. Her heart sinks to the floor when she discovers why they are there. She is panic-stricken and doesn't know what to do. On the one hand, they are offering her eleven hundred pieces of silver – from each ruler – if she will entice Samson enough to get him to tell her the secret of his strength. This was enough money to set herself up for life. She would never again be dependent on anyone else. Her future would definitely be secured, and she could face her old age with certainty. This is very important for her as a single woman, and without this financial security, she could be reduced to living on charitable handouts in her old age.

On the other hand, accepting their money and carrying out their plan would call for an act of great betrayal and deception towards a man she loves and adores very much. She knows that she would physically hurt inside to inflict that on Samson. However, that physical pain would never equal the emotional pain she would endure when she would see the look of disbelief in his eyes as he finally realises what she has done to him. She knows with a sick feeling in the pit of her stomach that after baring his soul to her, Samson will be shocked to learn that she would carry out such a devious act against him. Certainly, he would think that all along she had been reducing him to a place of emotional weakness to trap him more easily later. Her eyes welled up with tears and her heart ached just thinking about it.

Frantically Delilah's mind raced through the various options of how and when to betray Samson as she contemplated different scenarios. If she refused what these powerful men were offering her, there would definitely be repercussions. After all, look what happened to Samson's ex wife and father-in-law. They were both mercilessly burned in revenge for what Samson had done. The fact that he later avenged them by killing several other Philistines may have appeased him, but it could not bring back his wife and father-in-law.

Delilah wondered about something else, though: With all his might and power, could Samson actually protect her if she refused to help these Philistine rulers? After all, despite the fact that he had great strength and skill, he was still just one man. He was no match for the many armies that the Philistines could muster. In fact, there was no guarantee that he would even make it though the whole process alive, in which case Delilah would still be left alone and vulnerable.

Delilah was jolted back to reality as she realised that the five rulers were pressing her for an answer. She knew that she needed to think things through carefully. If she refused, it would not only have an impact on herself and Samson but on their extended families as well. The rulers would be angry and would waste no time in exacting their revenge on all

Just Want to be Loved for Me...

who stood in their way. They would have no qualms about wiping out whole generations if they needed to.

Delilah felt naked and vulnerable as the strength and covering she always got from Samson slipped down and fell to the floor. She felt helpless and greatly intimidated by these powerful men. Part of her wanted Samson to walk through the door that very second and destroy them all to protect her. Yet at the same time she wanted to protect and nurture the man she had grown to love and adore – the handsome, sensitive man who had given her the hope of a bright future after all that she had been through. This man had become her lover, her friend and her confidante, and she could not imagine life without him.

She knew that for all intents and purposes she was an innocent and disposable pawn in a very political arena. This was definitely a no-win situation. Whichever option she chose, she would be the loser. She felt the weight of her lowly position both as a mere woman with no rights and as a regular citizen at the mercy of the authorities. Her shoulders stooped and her posture slumped under the sheer pressure of it all.

Somewhere from within the depths of her spirit, she heard an almost inaudible voice agree with the terms that the rulers had offered her, and she realised that although it sounded like her voice responding to them, it did not represent what she wanted or who she really was.

The aftermath
After the Philistine rulers had left, Delilah went over the situation again and again. She even toyed with the idea of

telling Samson as soon as possible, and together they could decide what to do. Then at least she would not have to face this awful decision and carry this burden alone.

But the more she thought about telling Samson, the more she realised that was something she could never do. She knew him well enough by now to know that he would react out of great anger, hate and revenge, just as he had done to his enemies before he fell in love with Delilah. This would not solve the problem and would potentially make things worse. On top of this worry, Delilah was very nervous at the thought of crossing the Philistine rulers and facing their repercussions.

Deep down in her heart she knew it was all over between her and Samson. There seemed to be no way out. She cried bitter tears of regret, helplessness and hurt for what she was about to do. She also cursed the Philistines for destroying her only hope for happiness with a man she truly loved who genuinely loved her in return. Her only hope was that he would not be killed by the Philistines. She was a great believer in the old saying 'while there is life there is hope'. Who knows? Maybe there would be an opportunity for them to rebuild a life together later on, but if Samson were dead, there would be no such hope.

Delilah mentally began to prepare herself for the task ahead. This was not the time for tears or regret; she needed to focus intensely on what had to be done. The quicker it was all over the better, and then they could all move on with their lives.

Just Want to be Loved for Me...

Delilah executes her plan

Delilah sets herself to work immediately, and the very next time she and Samson are alone together she questions him about the secret of his strength as well as how best to overpower him. He appears to be blissfully unaware of her motives and does not even pick up on the fact that she has a sudden interest in his strength. He takes it as an opportunity to play around with her. He tells her that if he is bound with seven fresh bowstrings that have not yet been dried, he will become as weak as any other man.

The Philistine rulers provided her with the bowstrings for the next time she would be alone with Samson, and they set men in hiding in an inner room. Samson and Delilah always spent time together, waiting for the right moment to make their move. Delilah binds Samson with the bowstrings and calls out that the Philistines are there with them. Samson jumps up and responds immediately. He breaks the bowstrings as easily as a piece of yarn would break if it were to touch fire.

Delilah is furious and confronts him angrily. She accuses him of mocking her and again begs him to tell her the secret of his strength. He plays with her again and tells her that if he is bound with fresh new ropes that have never been used he will become as weak as any man and be unable to break free. Delilah again sets men in wait, hidden about the room. She binds Samson with the new ropes and calls out that the Philistines are there. Again, Samson jumps up and responds immediately, breaking free from the ropes as easily as if they were a piece of thread.

Delilah is getting anxious now and again angrily confronts him. She accuses him of telling lies in addition to mocking her. She insists that he now tell her the truth about his strength. Once again, he appears to be sorry for playing with her, and this time he tells her that if seven locks of his hair are woven into the web of the loom he will become weak. Delilah weaves his hair into the loom and then calls out that the Philistines are there among them. This time, even though he has fallen asleep, he jumps up out of his sleep and pulls his hair from the loom.

This is Delilah's third attempt to get Samson to tell her the secret of his strength. She is now getting more and more anxious and is worried that her plan may fail. She decides to change her tactics a little bit. This time she questions the strength of his love for her. She accuses him by saying that surely if he really loves her, he would not keep secrets from her. In addition to this, she reminds him that he has been lying to her and mocking her too.

Sometimes you cannot see what is right in front of you

It always amazes me that Samson fails to question Delilah or become suspicious of her sudden interest in the secret of his strength. Finding out what he says his weaknesses are has not proved enough for her either. She has bound him three separate times and has tested him each time. She has allowed him to believe that he is really under attack from the Philistines. Given all of this, he has not taken her seriously and has continued to view her challenges as some kind of game between them.

This reminds me that sometimes we fail to see the truth about certain situations or people even when it has manifested itself plainly to us and is staring us in the face. Often we are so blinded by what we think we know about another person that we close our minds to seeing the truth about them.

This is especially easy to do when our hearts are involved and we are blinded by love, as Samson seems to have been. He appears to be so consumed by his love for Delilah that he cannot bear to think an evil thought about her, and this gives her a level of power over him that is extremely potent and dangerous. He concentrates only on the positive aspects of their relationship. He focuses only on how much peace and joy she has brought to his heart. He still remembers how enthralled he was the first time he felt the soft silkiness of her hair as he ran his fingers through it and caressed it. His memory is littered with images of her scented, full figured body that has always longed for his touch.

There was the passion that always burned out of her sexy alluring eyes, ignited by a single look from him. All he could see was how good this woman was for him, and nothing else mattered. Maybe now she was just being a sly daring little fox as she played this game of wits with him.

On the other hand, it could have been that Samson was just as cunning and smart as Delilah was, and being the ultimate strong alpha male, he could afford to play with her a little and see how long she would keep up this game with him. He could see that she was vying for power in the relationship, looking for something that would give her the edge and that would indicate that they had reached a new level in how close they were. After all, when two people become as one, there are no physical or emotional barriers between them, and certainly no secrets.

The answers he gives her seem to be rather strange ones. They may indicate a belief in superstition, the supernatural, and in God, all at the same time. He refers to the number seven in two of the responses he gives to Delilah concerning his strength. This is a sacred number and is often associated with the notion of 'completion'. A good example of this is in Genesis chapter 1 where it tells us that God created everything in six days, and on the seventh day he rested because his work was complete.

When Samson told her that he could be held by fresh bowstrings, he was referring to the belief in some cultures of the era that bowstrings contained specials powers in their natural state. Nonetheless, they are made of unprocessed gut and are therefore not as strong as the seasoned ones. Samson was trying to give Delilah a hint by telling her this, but she didn't pick up on it because she was so intent on carrying out her plan.

Samson was also giving her a hint when he told her about weaving his hair. Again, there is a link to the superstitions of the day around the restraining of hair. The issue of the rope is a strange one, as there is no evidence to suggest that new rope is any stronger than rope that has never been used. It is also possible that this may have been linked to some myth or belief that was commonplace at that time.

A woman scorned

After three attempts to learn the secret of Samson's strength, Delilah is beside herself with worry and stress. The whole unpleasant business has dragged on for far too long now. In addition to that, she is feeling undermined at

Samson's continued reluctance to reveal his secret to her. This adds to her distress, and for the first time she seriously questions another aspect of his strength – that of his love for her.

Never mind the Philistines and what they wanted her to do; as a woman – Samson's woman no less – Delilah was beginning to feel scorned. After all, she had loved him unconditionally all this time. She had allowed him to completely and fully change her mind about men. For the first time in a long time, she had allowed herself to believe a man with all her heart when Samson said he loved her and wanted nothing more than to be with her for the rest of his life. Now it seemed that she could not rely on anything or anyone in her life. Aside from the political game she found herself embroiled in, she now had cause to doubt her man. She was depressed and felt that her life was over in more ways than one.

The famous bard, William Shakespeare, once wrote that 'hell hath no fury like a woman scorned', a saying that has become very famous, especially now in the modern day when we see women going to all sorts of extremes to secure revenge or to get justice over an errant man. At times like this, women appear to possess a level of genius in dealing with the issue that goes beyond how they might normally think on a daily basis when they are calmer. The gloves come off and women switch from being sweet, soft, lovable creatures to being highly manipulative and strategic. There are no boundaries when it comes to how far they'll go to quench their thirst to get even. They are able to come up with elaborate, innovative and highly sophisticated plans in a bid to get revenge on the unsuspecting men who have scorned them.

Women are women, and this one fact does not change over time. Therefore, their behaviour in Delilah's time was no different than it is now. In the book of Genesis chapter 3, we read not only of the fall of Adam and Eve, but also of the judgement that God hands down to them. Among other things, he tells Eve that 'your desire shall be for your husband and he shall rule over you'.

This is a very crucial scripture and tells us a lot about the essential nature of women. We women contain an almost untameable power within our very make up. It is so strong that if a woman is left to her own devices, this power can ultimately lead to very destructive behaviour on her part. Men were created by God to be our covering. With a good man's love and guidance, this power can be channelled into extremely positive energy. Under the protection of a man's covering, a woman will fulfil the purpose that she was created for.

Women make excellent leaders because of their ability to effect change through influence. We also have the uncanny ability to receive what we are given and then use it to produce something else. For example, a woman receives a seed from her husband and produces a child; she turns a house into a home by adding her own feminine touches; and she skilfully uses a whole list of ingredients to produce a fabulous meal. These are some of the positive aspects of a woman's ability to grow much increase from a seed. However, there is definitely an opposite side to this ability. Without the covering of a man, she may use her influential and creative powers to do other things that might not reflect positive attributes.

Just Want to be Loved for Me...

A woman will always naturally yearn towards her man. This means her desire will be for him. It is only because of this yearning that men are able to gain some level of control over women. A woman, in turn, will do anything to please her man and to keep things ticking over. As we have seen in this story about Delilah, however, a woman is able to switch gears in an instant if her position is abused or if she reaches the end of her patience with the man. Then the man is in the unenviable position of trying to reason with her when she is beyond the point of reason. He then has to manage the full backlash of her heated anger.

On a mission for the truth

Delilah changes her tactic and sets out to achieve her goal with single-minded focus. At this point, she has become so consumed by her feelings of anger and rejection that she decides to step up her assault on the poor unassuming Samson.

She tackles him again and again accusing him of deceiving her with lies. She plays the guilt trip card on him by accusing him of not honouring the precious love she thought they shared. She outwardly moans about the fact that she is now aware that she's been in a one-sided relationship all along. She accuses Samson by claiming there is no way that he could really love her the way she has loved him (even though she is the one who connived to trick him). After all, she proclaims, she has never lied to him, and she certainly has hidden no secrets from him. She cries constantly and remains bleary eyed and sullen most of the time.

She refuses to engage Samson in conversation about anything other than this matter. She is so desperately sad, and it pains Samson to see her this way. He hates to see her tears and desperately wants the situation to be over with. He is mortified to realise that she cannot be reasoned with. He also cannot believe that she no longer responds to his winning smiles or his smoky seductive eyes that, even in her stubborn anger, threaten to ravish her whole body right there on the spot. In fact, whenever he tries to force the issue she either sullenly pushes him away or remains stiff as a board in his arms. She refuses to give him eye contact, and she feels like a stranger in his presence.

Samson begins to feel under threat and does not quite know how to handle the situation. He asks himself over and over again why women have to be so difficult. He is also annoyed for letting himself be so deeply affected by her. After all, he was Samson the hero. He was able to have any woman at his beck and call, and he still could if he wanted to. However, there was only one woman that he loved and desired with all his heart. She was able to wrap him around her little finger and he was powerless to stop her or even to walk away.

He found himself pining for her desperately and longed with all his heart to hear her mischievous laughter and to feel her soft warm body that was always so pliable under his touch.

Delilah was a woman on a mission, and she was not about to give up without achieving her goal. She carried out her assault for days on end until Samson was weary and miserable. She knew the victory would be hers if she could manage to hold on for long enough. After all, this

Just Want to be Loved for Me...

was exactly what his ex wife had done to him when she had sought to get the answer to the riddle Samson had posed at their wedding. Delilah knew that this was Samson's main weak point, and she would use it to her full advantage.

As time went by Delilah also began to feel the strain. She was not coping well being at constant loggerheads with him. She too deeply missed their moments of intimacy and their constant companionship. In any event, the Philistine rulers were still waiting for her news. She was convinced that there would be a breakthrough any time now and so was loath to give up on accomplishing her goal. She felt like there was no choice; she would simply have to wait until he gave in.

Persistence pays off

Eventually things reach a crisis point and Delilah is on the verge of giving in. Before she can get a chance to act on her resolve, Samson finally breaks down. He is sick and tired of the constant silences broken only by Delilah's tearful accusations. He longs for her with an enhanced feeling of passion brought on by the pent up frustrations and awkwardness of the situation. He misses her and desperately wants everything to return to normal. He longs to see Delilah smile again, and to drink in her deep, loving eyes as she clung to him.

At one point, Samson comes to Delilah and tells her that he wants to talk. She feels her heart race a little because she knows that he is about to tell her everything. He is fed up with the whole mess. This is aptly described in the Bible when it states that his soul is 'vexed to death' by the situation (see verse 16).

Samson now bares his soul to Delilah telling her all she wants to hear. He breaks down all barriers in a bid to appease the woman he loves. Finally, they can truly be as one and move on together in their relationship.

He explains about his special birth and the fact that as a Nazirite his hair has never been touched by a razor. He confirms at last that if his head were shaved, he would become as weak and vulnerable as any other ordinary man. Something about the way he speaks with such intensity assures Delilah that this time he is telling the truth. She cannot believe that he has shared his innermost thoughts and secrets with her. Now she is certain that he truly does love her, and this makes her next steps so much more difficult to carry out.

She goes over the events in her mind again and again feeling such a sense of peace and calm. She basks in the ambience of the renewed love and fervour in their relationship. She senses that now their love is reaching a new level, and this gives her much joy, but that joy is mingled with the bittersweet pain of knowing what she has to do next.

She weighs up the different options available to her, and still she is at a loss as to how to get the two of them out of this situation. There seems to be no other way out, so she leaves Samson relaxing in the house while she goes to tell the Philistines what he has told her about the secret to his strength. Of course, they are elated to hear her news; finally, they can bring about their plan! So they immediately get up and follow her home.

Just Want to be Loved for Me...

Delilah goes inside alone and acts as though nothing has changed. She and Samson revel in each other's company and enjoy talking about all the good times they've spent together. They share a glass of wine together. It is with a heavy heart that Delilah spikes his glass with something to make him sleepy. Afterwards they recline together with Samson's head comfortably placed on her lap, one of his favourite positions. They speak together lovingly while Delilah strokes his temples and his hair. He always found it so peaceful and relaxing being with her. She knew just how to make a man feel good.

It is not long before he drifts off into a peaceful sleep. Delilah lies there still for a good while to make sure that he is truly asleep, and while she waits, she takes some time to contemplate the irreversible chain of events that are about to unfold.

She hopes that this time she has managed to get the truth from him and that the whole thing will soon be over. The strain had taken a toll on her both emotionally and physically. She simply could not bear for this to be another false start. If so, she would be forced to keep at him until his resolve finally broke. Delilah looked down at Samson and watched his peaceful sleeping form. She stroked and fondled his hair lovingly and could not believe that she had not guessed his secret before. This was her time to savour her memories of the man she loved and adored. She silently said goodbye to him before signalling the men waiting outside to come in and shave Samson's head.

Samson is disarmed

Once it was done, the men stepped back while Delilah shouted out once again that the Philistines were there. Samson was slower waking up this time, and he was decidedly groggy at first. Delilah knew that this was because of the drug she had mixed into his drink beforehand. As soon as Samson realised that the men were in fact waiting in the room for him, he rose angrily to attack them. He stopped short very suddenly as he noticed hair scattered on the floor all around him. While he stared in shocked disbelief, he was attacked by one of the men, and instead of meeting the onslaught with his usual brute force, he stumbled immediately, shocked at his inability to fight back. The men realised at once that Samson was indeed weak now and they easily subdued him.

Delilah stood helplessly by watching as they bound him as a prisoner, this man she loved who was now a shell of his former glorious being. His bewildered eyes sought hers looking for some kind of explanation for what was taking place. The men began to cheer and make rude comments about him as they praised Delilah for bringing this brute to justice. He quickly realised that Delilah had played a part in orchestrating the events. He also saw her being given her reward by the Philistines who were overjoyed with her work. The Philistines were now ready to take Samson away to prison.

He looked around the room mentally taking a note of everything in it, storing away the memories he would need for the endless days and nights that awaited him in prison. He felt numbed with shock and disbelief that his own dear sweet Delilah could have betrayed him to his sworn enemies

Just Want to be Loved for Me...

the Philistines. He felt sure that he was missing a crucial part of the puzzle that would allow him to make sense of what was going on. Could it be that she had never loved him at all? He berated himself immediately; of course she loved him and always had. He remembered her eyes so full of love and adoration, and her passionate kisses and how she clung to him with all her might when they made love. His mind drew a blank.

He was utterly shocked at this turn of events – this outright betrayal by Delilah. Nonetheless, whatever had happened, he was not going to find out right now. He prepared himself to be led away like a lamb to the slaughter. His body felt weak and limp, a strange feeling he had never experienced before. Even his steps felt laboured as he stumbled towards the door.

Suddenly a loud commanding voice shouted for him to stop. It was the voice of one of the Philistines who had come to witness the event. He ordered the men to bring Samson back to the centre of the room. To the amazement of everyone there, he made an order for Samson's eyes to be put out. This would put the final icing on the cake for them. It would also reduce Samson's present and future ability to make any impact on his enemies.

Delilah gasped outwardly in shock and horror. Surely, she had misheard the order. This had never been mentioned before. She had always understood that he would be captured and imprisoned to make sure that he could never create havoc for the Philistines again. She opened her mouth to protest but was quickly threatened and silenced by the guards. She began to weep uncontrollably, begging for mercy for Samson and offering to give her reward money back to them. They would not be moved, and she watched helplessly as they used a heated sword to blind him. His screams resounded and echoed throughout every room of the house and beyond. Each decibel cut into Delilah's heart like a sharp knife searing her flesh. She collapsed into a crumpled heap, sobbing and shaking uncontrollably.

Delilah tries to move on

Delilah felt betrayed by the Philistines' final act of cruelty in blinding Samson. It had caused the light to go out in the windows of Samson's soul, forcing him to live in a world of darkness, away from his people and from everything he knew and loved. Delilah was inconsolable and beside herself with grief. Her hopes of him being released one day and being able to live out his days with her were now gone. In a single instant, it had all been over, and she knew for certain that things could never be the same between them. She blamed herself over and over for choosing to conspire with the Philistines against her beloved Samson.

Deep down, she knew the choices available to her were very limited, each one fraught with its own difficulties and complications. She visualised his face smiling at her and the way his eyes had always twinkled when he laughed, especially when she teased him. How she longed for everything to be the way it always had been between them. She was not even allowed to see him when she went to the prison begging for just a few minutes alone with him. She hurt all over and had not slept in such a long time. She had lost so much weight, her eyes were red and puffy, and in many ways, the light had gone out in her soul too. She tried to be pragmatic about the whole thing, but right now all she could feel was hate and anger for everything and everyone, including herself.

Just Want to be Loved for Me...

Delilah felt an undeniable urge to be near the things Samson loved so much, including his people, and so she went to the area where he used to live. Not surprisingly, his family refused to see her, and she was suddenly aware that she was probably the most hated woman in the area. Everyone blamed her completely for the loss of the great man who had been their people's champion, their hero and their judge. People called her nasty names and shunned her.

Other men were too afraid to approach her or be associated with her. She was a marked woman. Songs were written and sung about her alluding to how she had used her beauty and sexuality to trap and destroy the hero. Little girls were warned about the dangers of being like Delilah and were pressured into mending their ways if they were showing tendencies toward being 'Delilahs' – yes, even her name had now become synonymous with 'that kind' of woman.

No one cared enough about her to hear her side of the story. They had already made up their minds. No one even considered her reasoning as valid or saw the sincerity of her silent cries as she wept for all that she had lost, especially the man who had loved her with all his heart. Delilah didn't blame them for hating and judging her; she didn't much like herself either. She would always be remembered as the scarlet woman that caused Samson to lose it all.

It was all made worse by the fact that Samson's hair did in fact grow back eventually, and his strength returned along with it. One day while he was being paraded in the temple dedicated to Dagon, the Philistine god, he asked to be placed between the two main pillars that supported the temple. They had no idea why he made this specific request, but

Samson knew. He asked God to strengthen him one more time so that he could exact his revenge on the Philistines and die with them. God heard his prayer, and while the people laughed and jeered at him again and again, taunting him about his lack of strength (or so they thought), Samson pushed the pillars away. The temple collapsed, killing nearly all the people who were gathered there. It was the end of Samson and the final straw for Delilah.

Right from the start, when she had first been approached by the Philistines, she had known deep down that their proposition would end up being a doomed situation for all involved. There would be no winners, least of all her. The money performed its function and enabled her to live comfortably for the rest of her life, but it could never replace or bring back the man she had loved with all her heart and but who she had betrayed so cruelly.

Now she knew what it was like to be a mere woman with no rights, subject to the whim of others. She was treated as a disposable pawn in a large political arena. After all, she was *just* a woman.

Modern day Delilahs

Despite the fact that 'Delilah' is not a name readily chosen for little girls, it still has the power to strike a chord at the heart of every girl's life. Decent girls will do everything they can to avoid being likened to her. The name still denotes shame and distaste, and women like Delilah are still not taken seriously.

As shown through this close examination of her life and character, Delilah was a warm-hearted woman who was not

Just Want to be Loved for Me...

only used by powerful men to weaken the man she loved, but who forever became the original 'Miss understood'. Very few people take the time to read her entire story in the Bible and discover what she was really like. In many ways, she has even been dehumanised and portrayed as cold and hard. Most people are happy to believe what they have heard about Delilah without seeking the truth for themselves.

Lots of women today are misunderstood and painted with all sorts of bad labels. It is important to understand that people always have a reason for everything they do. They make their choices and decisions based on what they have been subject to. For example, a woman who has been subject to abuse in her early life may not be able to place a high value on the sacredness of her body. When she freely gives her body to others, she is accused of being loose and cheap. She is easily judged and often shunned. Most people don't take the time to get to know her and understand the pain in her past that still drives her every decision in the present and into the future (unless she can find healing).

The male partners of these women often portray them very negatively, particularly after a break-up in the relationship. The men will have their listeners sympathetically thinking that he has done well to escape from the clutches of such an evil woman. It is important to remember, however, that there are always two sides to a coin, and people are often surprised to learn the woman's version of the story, and will possibly even change their opinion of her when they really hear what she has to say.

Like Delilah, women sometimes find themselves in situations where they must choose the lesser of two evils. It may well be the case that a woman's initial poor choices are what put her in the bad situation in the first place. This does not mean that she is not a victim or is not worthy of support and sympathy. It is often the case that people fall into situations innocently without being aware of the serious implications and repercussions those situations will have.

The Delilahs of today may be the victims of their circumstances, and their behaviour is simply a reaction to the inherent need to protect themselves. There is the girl who seems to use men heartlessly to get what she wants, but on closer inspection, we find that she has been used and abandoned by men, and she refuses now to give her heart away.

There is also the girl with a boyfriend her parents hate. She becomes pregnant only to be rejected by her family, and then on top of that, later she finds out that her boyfriend is a drug dealer. Unable to go back home she ends up living on the proceeds of crime. This becomes her life until she can no longer remember what life was like before.

Or how about the girl who, anxious to show that she can cope on her own, leaves an unhappy home to find freedom, and even when life becomes impossibly hard she just soldiers on. She cannot face returning home with her tail between her legs. With her dreams in shreds, she ends up in prostitution, living in a drug-induced haze just to get herself through the daily pain of survival.

In all these scenarios, what other people see on the surface is a loser who appears to have opted out of life. It often seems that people make up their minds about certain girls based on the labels that have been applied to them. They will seldom open up their hearts to these girls and really hear their side of the story. Forgiveness is not readily given, and the girls are ostracised or insulted.

In turn, the girls become hardened to what other people say or think about them. They become numbed to the pain of never being quite good enough, and they learn to ignore the distasteful looks of disapproval. They no longer cringe when they hear people warning younger women about the dangers of becoming like them. They find other ways to become socially accepted. After a time they in turn will reject the women who follow the norm. They will snigger and turn their noses up at the perfect little goody-goodies with their boring straight-laced lives.

Take hope

If you are misunderstood as Delilah was, please know that it doesn't really matter what anyone else thinks about you or your life. The truth is that God is the one who created you, and he knows all there is to know about you, including all that you have suffered and endured. There are no secrets with him; he is your loving heavenly Father, and there is no need to have pretensions when you are pouring your heart out to him in private.

It is not clear whether Delilah even knew God or whether she was able to call on him during her darkest moments, but it doesn't have to be this way for you.

Today you can call on God at any time. He hears all your prayers, and contrary to popular opinion, he did not send his son Jesus to save the righteous only. Jesus came to save all of us no matter who we are, what we have done or where we have come from.

God created everyone for a purpose, and it is up to each person to answer the call and move into her or his destiny. This includes you! In fact, you have more in common with Jesus than many other people do. He too was talked about, and not always in a favourable way. Even when he tried to do good things, he was rejected. People always misunderstood his actions and his motives. People often tried to trick him into saying things that could be used as evidence against him or further discredit him. In spite of all that he had done to show his love and care for people, such as feeding them and healing them, many people still turned against him. At the end of it all, he was ultimately put to death having committed no crime.

Make that change today

You need to remember that Jesus endured all of this for you personally. He loved you so much that he was willing to endure whatever was thrown at him and to pay the ultimate price of death on a cross. This was to ensure that when the time came, **you** would have a way out. As Jesus put it so simply, "I am the way, the truth, and the life; no one comes to the Father except by me" (John 14:6).

I hear you asking yourself, *well, this all sounds good, but what does it mean for me in real terms? On a practical level, what do I need to do?*

Salvation is not a complicated process, contrary to how some religious organisations teach it. You do not need to dress weirdly, talk with a new vocabulary, or make a drastic change and become a clone of what you think a Christian looks like.

God created you, and he loves you just as you are, with all your flaws, your wonderful personality, your sense of adventure and fun. Most of all, he loves the way you love to experiment with different looks for your hair, clothes and make up. He wants nothing more than to have a one-to-one relationship with you so that you can begin to walk into the purpose and destiny he created you for.

Come to him just as you are. Do not give in to the pressure from others who say that you have to drastically change or else you will not be accepted by God. There is bound to be a church in your community that will accept you as you are without condemnation. Remember, once you decide to let God into your life, he will take over, and whatever changes need to be made in you, **he** will make them as you grow in him. You only need to be flexible in your spirit and be willing to be led by him through his Holy Spirit.

I have often come across dedicated Christians who constantly struggle to give up their addictions to cigarettes, cannabis, pornography, illicit sexual behaviour and any number of habits that control their lives. If they were to wait to be healed before they came to God, they would probably never make it. God wants them (and you) to come to him just as you are, but the enemy will try to convince you otherwise and make you think you are not worthy enough to belong to God's family.

Some people have been healed of their addictions within seconds, minutes and days. Others struggle for years before they are delivered. You just need to trust God and carry on no matter what. Be encouraged that all of the people in your local church are struggling with some kind of 'sinful' or challenging behaviour. Just because you may not see it or hear them talk about it does not mean it's not there.

I remember being so touched to hear a testimony of an ex convict who finally managed to give his life to Christ. He told of how he grew spiritually from strength to strength. However, he was unable to give up smoking cannabis, which he had been smoking for the last twenty years. Despite many sessions of prayer and fasting, it remained a thorn in his side. He was filled with guilt and remorse each time he smoked, but still he could not manage to give it up. After two years he went home from a prayer meeting one night, took out a joint to smoke it, and just as he was about to light it, he heard a voice. It asked him why he needed to do it, and he answered, "To give me peace before I sleep." The voice said, *Isn't my peace enough to keep you?* The words convicted him deep down in his spirit. He put down the joint and never touched another one again.

Salvation

There are four easy steps you need to follow if you want God to take over your life and lead you into the destiny he created you for.

1. **Believe**
   Believe with all your heart that Jesus is the son of God, and that he came to earth to be an example to us and to die for our sins. Believe that because he made this sacrifice, you now have the chance to be saved through his grace and to live with him in eternity.

2. **Repent of your sins**
   This means being genuinely sorry and asking God to forgive you, to change your life, and to show you how to live for him.

3. **Be baptised in water**
   This is an outward sign to the world that you have decided to change your life by accepting Jesus as your Lord and Saviour. At some point, you will also be baptised with the gift of the Holy Spirit. He will live within you, guide you and help you throughout the ups and downs of life.

4. **Begin a relationship with God**
   The way you do this is by getting to know him and learning all you can about him. You can do this by praying and talking to him, by praising him with singing and clapping your hands, and by giving him your tithes and offerings. You should also read the Bible to find out all about him. You will learn all about the heart and character of God by reading his living Word, including the things he likes and dislikes concerning us, his children, and the things he wants us to do.

You will also learn about his intentions when he created you and the earth. You will share in knowing his ultimate plans for the world, and how those plans will be manifested in modern life. Most valuable of all is that you will have a reference guide at your fingertips to help you to live your life the way he intended you to.

Don't be surprised to find that the Bible has something to say on almost everything. The topics are as far reaching as science, philosophy, history, finance, relationships and death, covering the range of every emotional and spiritual state you can think of. Make sure you check it out!

Finally

Right now, Jesus knows better than anyone else what you have been through. He knows your pain and how much you have tried to pretend that it really doesn't matter. A woman's sensuality does not have to be a curse. He knows the real you. Know within yourself that there are options, and yes, they are open to ***you***. Go ahead, take that step … make that change now. May your life become abundantly rich in all areas as you find him and discover the real you that he lovingly create you to be.

Chapter Eight

The Ultimate Plan 'B'

Eve's Story

Introduction

It took me a long time to write this final chapter because I knew I wanted it to be all about Eve. I struggled to find the right angle from which to tell her story. After all, Eve is one of the most talked about and most written about women of all time.

Everyone has heard of her, and everyone has their own opinion of who they think she was or what she actually did. In addition, she has been blamed for being the bearer of sin and being responsible for the fallen world we live in. This has led to women being viewed negatively, for the most part. We are often cursed as 'daughters of Eve' or laughed at and regaled for our gullibility and stupidity.

In this chapter, I want to consider a number of themes and explore how these may have impacted the lives of modern women. (For its Bible reference, the full story of Eve is found in the book of Genesis, from chapter 2 verse 21 on through the next few chapters.)

The story begins

We read very early on in Genesis that, having created all things, including Adam, the first man, God decides that it is not good for Adam to be alone. He decides to create a woman to be a helpmate for Adam. God does this by causing Adam to fall into a deep sleep and removing one of his ribs. In creating the woman, God was creating a very special being. She was not an afterthought. In fact, many people refer to her as the 'crown of creation'. At that point, she was most definitely the final touch to six days of perfect creation. In the beginning, she was called 'Ishah', which in Hebrew means 'woman'. This is interpreted by some as meaning 'a man with a womb'. Afterwards, Adam named her 'Eve', which means 'life bearer'.

It is important to remind ourselves that Eve was created in the Garden from Adam's rib. This relates to her intended position. She was to be his helpmate, and she would take a strong role in helping him carry out the purpose that God had created both of them for. She was not taken from Adam's head to be above him or from his feet to be under him. She was instead taken from his side to work alongside him. They would both operate as equals but would carry out different functions and have distinctive but complementary traits. It is also interesting to note that unlike Eve, who was created in the Garden of Eden, Adam was created outside of the Garden in the wild. Later God placed him in the Garden to look after it.

We should also remember that Adam was asleep when Eve was created. He was therefore not privy to how God made her or how she was to function. The woman was presented to him as a complete being. Now that she was his wife, there would be plenty of opportunities for Adam to discover her mysteries: her unique likes and dislikes, and her secret entrances that led to the inner core of her body. He would also learn how to tap into, affect and influence her emotional being. These secrets would be for their mutual excitement and pleasure, and would create a lasting, personal, intimate bond between them. As well as the relationship between them, they would also enjoy a personal one-to-one relationship with God, their creator. This was truly the perfect world.

Just Want to be Loved for Me...

Learning the rules

We are told that God created all things and that both Adam and Eve were free to enjoy and partake of all that was in the Garden. They spent time together simply basking in each other's company and their awesome surroundings. They also worked hard tending and taking care of the Garden. Before Eve was even created, God clearly told Adam that he could eat from every tree in the Garden except from the tree of the knowledge of good and evil. God told him that the day Adam ate of it he would 'surely die' (Genesis 3:17).

The truth was that being barred from eating of this one tree did not create a hardship for Adam and Eve. The Garden was enormous and beautiful with so many kinds of flowers, plants, shrubs and fruit trees. In addition, there were ample varieties of delicious and luscious fruits, nuts, berries and plants to eat without getting bored with the same diet every day.

The beauty of the Garden gave them so many opportunities to witness and revel in the glory of God's different creations. There was nothing left to chance or created as an afterthought. Each thing was special in its own way and was specifically designed with its purpose in mind. For example, brightly coloured petals were designed to attract and draw insects to land on them and thus transfer pollen so the flowers could reproduce themselves. From the tiniest creations to the largest creatures so perfectly formed and equipped to fit into their environment where they would live and eat. Whether it was to be under a rock, in the trees or in the earth, they had been created so that everything they needed to function was close by or within easy reach.

Both Adam and Eve lived at one with the Garden, the creatures and the elements, and of course with God. Between them, they knew every living thing that they lovingly cared for and that Adam had named. In particular, Eve had her favourites, although she loved all things. She was especially thrilled by the fact that she was able to enjoy all things in their seasons. There were the evergreen varieties that stayed green all year and that could be enjoyed at any time. Then there were the seasonal plants that signalled the beginning or ending of the seasons. She looked forward to the daffodils that peeped shyly out of their buds at the start of springtime. Later on, she looked forward to when the roses would be in full bloom. Their perfumed aroma permeated the Garden and filled the air with their sweet scent.

Eve was always sad when she saw their petals begin to wilt and to bow down toward the earth. She knew that this signalled the beginning of the end of summer. Later she would witness their beauty as they lay littered like confetti on the ground and at the foot of the stem. Afterwards they would curl at the ends, dry up and be blown away by the wind. They would disappear as quickly as they had come, having completed the purpose they were made for.

Evil steps in

One day as both Adam and Eve wandered through the Garden, they were joined by the serpent. He was created as an upright creature and was able to stand tall with his long body coiled into a heap on the ground. He greeted Eve and, as usual, she was happy to see him. He had become one of her best friends and they had often spent time together in the garden.

Just Want to be Loved for Me...

Today he was on a mission. He struck up a conversation with Eve, talking about all her favourite topics. This was why she liked him so much. They seemed to have so much in common and she was always able to learn interesting things from him. He never ceased to remind her jokingly that he was her elder because he had been created long before her. He was always able to make her laugh with his funny stories about the other creatures. He was definitely a trusted friend, and he often kept her company when Adam was busy tending the Garden.

As they walked around and talked, they came into the area where the tree of the knowledge of good and evil stood. Adam was weeding the flowerbeds and checking the leaves of the plants nearby. He mentally dipped in and out of their conversation and was happy that Eve was being amused by the serpent.

This left him able to focus on the work at hand. He preferred to work in silence, which meant that he often found it difficult to concentrate on the task at hand when Eve needed to talk to him. Being a typical man, he was not able to multi-task very well, no matter how many times Eve tried to teach him. He liked to do one thing at a time. He hated ignoring Eve because he knew that she depended on him a lot for company. He just could not understand how she managed to do so many things at once and still remember all the finer details involved. He could always rely on her to do whatever he asked of her, even if he approached her while she was engrossed in taking care of the flowers, chatting with one of the creatures or mentally making a note of all the other things she had to do that day.

The temperature was climbing as the full heat of the midday sun came to rest directly over the Garden. Adam paused to wipe the sweat from his brow. He looked over to where Eve and the serpent were talking. Eve looked so radiantly beautiful in the glow of the sun. He loved her with all his heart and had done since the moment God gave her to him. He had never before seen a creature so delicate and exquisite. Yet she possessed a quiet strength as she worked with him side by side. In one sense, she was so different to him and yet at the same time she was exactly like him. Her unique qualities were hard to describe in words, but they always filled him with an overwhelming sense of longing and need of her.

He admired her from afar as she relaxed in the serpent's company. He heard her giggle and then laugh out loud at something the serpent said to her. She looked so happy. His heart melted; she was everything to him – his wife, his family, his all. She was bone of his bone and flesh of his flesh and he loved everything about her. He loved her melodious laugh, the way she talked, and the way she teased him. He even loved the way she pouted when he didn't agree with her and refused to let her have her own way. Most of all he loved the fact that this woman loved and adored him too.

Adam was jolted back to the present when he heard the serpent mention the 'tree of the knowledge of good and evil'. He began to listen in earnest. Eve, too, was now extremely focused on what the serpent was saying. She had never mentioned it to anyone before. In fact, she had never even discussed it with Adam. God had made the rules very clear about not eating from it, and they had accepted and understood those rules without question, knowing that God always wanted the best for them.

Just Want to be Loved for Me...

The serpent asked Eve whether it was true that God had told them not to eat the fruit from that tree. Eve affirmed that it was so and confidently added that God had also said that the day they ate the fruit they would surely die. The serpent feigned complete shock and utter surprise. He told Eve that he could not believe that God had actually told them that. He assured her that it was most certainly not true. Eve maintained her position and could not be moved. She completely trusted God, and it had never occurred to her to question or doubt anything he told them, as he always had their best interest in mind.

The serpent was not to be put off from his mission that easily. He spent a large amount of time telling her why he was right. He reminded her again and again that he was the elder of the two and that he obviously knew things that she didn't know. He also told her that God had only told them they would die because he knew that if they did eat from the tree, their eyes would be opened and they would become like gods. They would know so many eternal truths, the serpent persuaded, especially all there was to know about good and evil.

Eve was not to be swayed, and as the serpent ranted on and on at her she became slightly annoyed and irritated with him. Despite being one of her best friends, he always behaved as if he knew so much about so many things. This always made her feel less intelligent and somehow very juvenile. Eventually he walked away after seeing that she would not budge on her stance.

The seed is sown

After he was gone, she mulled over the serpent's suggestions in her mind and promptly dismissed them. There was just no part of her that would believe anything the serpent said over what God had told them. Unknown to her, this was exactly what the serpent had planned from the start. He knew that Eve would reject his theories completely out of hand. What he also knew (but what she did not realise) was that the serpent had successfully planted a seed of doubt in her mind.

Adam had never responded to the serpent when he heard his theory. He refused to entertain the idea or to even allow the serpent to talk about it in his presence. His resolve was firm, and the serpent knew without a shadow of a doubt that he would never get to Adam directly. Therefore, he had turned his full attention to Eve. Her gentle sweet nature would never allow her to be rude enough to dismiss him from her presence.

Although the serpent continued to nurture and develop the friendship between them, he never missed an opportunity to bring up the tree whenever he could. In fact, it became a little bit of a joke between them, and whenever he mentioned it and saw Eve's perfectly beautiful face crease up with a worried frown, he would throw his arms up in mock surrender and apologise. The serpent had a certain charm and appeal that he knew Eve could not resist. It was cheeky and they both knew it. Yet Eve's ire was always disarmed by his infectious laughter and feigned surrender.

Eventually Eve found herself thinking about the powers of the tree more and more. The seeds of doubt strategically

Just Want to be Loved for Me...

placed in her mind by the serpent were now firmly taking hold, and she found herself questioning her thoughts and beliefs about whether or not it even mattered if she obeyed God and stayed away from the tree as he had commanded. She found herself asking whether the serpent could actually be right. If that were the case, then how wonderful it would be to be like God and to know all things.

She often found herself wandering in the area where the tree stood just so that she could gaze at it and ponder what the serpent had told her. She would sometimes just stand and stare at it. She had developed a firm picture in her mind of exactly what it looked like. It was a large attractive tree with many leafy branches bearing downwards by the weight of the ripe fruit. The fruit itself was perfectly shaped, and she found herself wondering what it would taste like. She fantasised that the flesh inside would be firm to the touch, yet luscious and juicy as its sweetness passed down her throat. She rejected the thought almost as soon as she entertained it and brought herself back to reality.

I am reminded of how this is also the way the enemy works on us today. He strategically knows every one of our weaknesses and feeds the ideas into our minds that will prey on those. This happens so subconsciously that we are often not even aware that we are receiving input from the enemy.

We take in all kind of thoughts, suggestions and ideas from a variety of sources. The most common are the television, radio, Internet, books and magazines. This is in addition to influences from school, church and even our family and friends. We mentally sift through all the information and decide which elements to believe and which to throw out.

We are more likely to keep the data that relates to things we naturally have a weakness for. The real danger is that if we do not dismiss and throw out the images or suggestions immediately, they will take a foothold in our mind and spirit. Once these ideas take a foothold in our mind, they can grow to the point where we will be tempted to act on them. This makes it more difficult to deal with these issues later because by that point, they have become part of us.

For example, when a woman sees a man she quite fancies, she usually begins wondering whether he would make a good husband. This may be irrespective of the fact that he has not even shown an interest in her yet. The more she sees of him, the more she thinks about him. He may even seem to become more appealing in her eyes, thereby occupying more time and space in her mind. This innocent thinking may begin to combine itself with other suggestions and feelings, particularly feelings of desire compounded by her loneliness and need of a good man.

These fantasies may lead her to become more and more aware of his physical characteristics. After a time she may start to wonder what it would be like to be intimate with him. Ultimately, she starts to visualise herself engaged in intimate relations with him. A woman in this state is more likely to become vulnerable to this man's charm if he approaches her. In many ways, she has already started the relationship in her mind. She may already have gone past the stage where she would normally be able to identify his negative attributes, which would then enable her to walk away from him.

Just Want to be Loved for Me...

Overcoming evil in our lives

When Jesus taught his disciples (and therefore all of us) to pray the Lord's Prayer, he included the line 'lead us not into temptation but deliver us from evil'. This is because he knew that we are not able to deliver ourselves. In fact, we need help to resist temptation every single day. The kind of thinking I've described above seems harmless enough, but it can lead us to the point where we act on our thoughts. People of God are called upon to resist evil in all its forms. This means rejecting it as soon as it enters your mind. This all sounds easy enough as a practical solution to the problem. However, in real terms it is one of the hardest things to do. Evil is able to present itself in many different forms. It is sometimes difficult to recognise it in its most subtle guises. Sin is sin whether it is blatant or not, and we need to guard ourselves against it at all times.

This is especially true when we are not fully aware of the consequences that might result from giving in to sin. One of the most effective ways to handle temptation is to consciously reject and dismiss the sinful thoughts, ideas or suggestions as soon as we become aware of them. Then, it is very important for us to fill our minds with thoughts that will prevent us from wandering back (mentally and literally) to the very things that we are trying to forget.

If you feel overwhelmed at the thought of conquering temptation on your own, please don't despair. You are not alone. It has been well established that trying to overcome evil on your own is almost impossible to do. Take proactive steps to 'think on things from above' as the Bible says. Once you have dismissed the tempting thought, fill your mind with praise. Begin to sing, clap, and worship, or take some time to pray. You can even decide to listen to your favourite Christian praise songs or read your Bible. A fully active and engaged mind is not able to nurture and develop negative thoughts. In addition, you need to talk to God and to ask him to deliver you from this temptation. Turn the situation over to him and he will be a very present help in your time of trouble.

If you make a conscious effort to follow these steps, only good can come of it. Firstly, it is a good habit to develop, and as you choose to pray, read the Bible and praise God, it will become a natural response to temptation. Secondly, each time you worship or pray it brings you closer to God. He never grows tired of hearing from you, and you will find that all kinds of blessings are released into your life as a result of staying in close communication with him.

Eve entertains the serpent's temptation

Even though Eve rejected the serpent's temptation when he first suggested it to her, she put herself in danger by allowing the concept to re-enter her mind again and again. The serpent's constant reinforcement allowed the thought to take root and grow in Eve's mind. Eventually she found herself going out of her way to be in a place where she could actually see the tree and think about its qualities, all the time giving the serpent's ideas space to develop in her mind. She did not know it at the time, but she was losing the battle inch by inch.

For his part, the serpent could not have been happier. He gleefully watched and was elated to see Eve's resolve begin to melt. His plan was working so well. He was good at persuasion and manipulation and he knew it. He realised that he did not even have to work so hard anymore to convince Eve.

The seed of doubt and curiosity had been sown and was growing very nicely, thank you very much. All he had to do was to wait and always be on hand to reinforce it if need be. He was still very much Eve's friend, and she was so naïve that she still could not see what was right in front of her very eyes. After all, she had never been exposed to the concept of deception before. Eve heavily relied on the serpent as a friend. She could not see that the relationship was one sided, that his motives were not genuine and that his intentions were flawed.

The serpent knew Eve better than she knew herself. He understood why God had created her and that she was a helpmate for Adam. In terms of her relationship with Adam, the serpent knew that Eve was the one with the power to influence her surroundings and her partner. The only question was whether she would choose to use her position for good or whether she could be persuaded to use it for evil. The serpent had known all along that if he managed to get through to Eve, then he definitely had a road in to reach Adam.

Eve finally gives in

One fateful day, all three of them were passing the time together in the area around ***that*** tree. Eve was at the point where she wanted to transpose what she had been thinking into reality. She was going to taste that fruit from the tree and see what really happened. It would be so good to become like a god. She would be smart and would know so much. She would never again feel like the most junior creation, with everyone around her knowing far more than she did. They had always been willing to pull rank as a reminder of her position.

It is strange to think of Eve feeling like this, but then, women have always struggled with issues of inferiority and self-esteem, and we have always put the needs of others before our own. Could it be possible that this inherent aspect of our nature stems from the thinking of our first mother, Eve? It is interesting to see how the serpent had managed to turn something so positive – the glory of Eve's creation – into something so negative. Instead of realising that she was the jewel in the crown of man and the icing on the cake of all the creatures on earth, she was now feeling quite low because she had been treated as an inferior person, a junior partner, so to speak. She was willing to risk everything she had to change that.

Eve felt nervous and fearful; her mouth and lips were suddenly dry and bereft of moisture. She licked her lips nervously as she weighed up the situation for the last time. She desperately sought to address any last minute nagging doubts as to whether she could really carry out what she planned to do.

Eve was responding now to the prospect of being like God and knowing all things. She paid very little attention to the prospect of dying as a consequence of her actions. In truth, she did not even know what the word 'dying' meant, and she had no concept of what dying might do to her. Somewhere in the dark recesses of her mind, she knew that it would *not* be a pleasant experience.

Just Want to be Loved for Me...

By this stage, however, the prospect of doing something that she knew was wrong was so strong that she couldn't overcome it. In fact, the more she thought about it, the more she realised that God had never explained what he meant when he said they would die if they ate of the fruit of this particular tree. For some reason this made her a little angry; *who is he to give us a command and not even explain why*, she wondered. Mentally she had processed her way through all the risk analysis scenarios in her mind. At the start of it all she had been shocked at the very thought of committing the sin, and now she was rationalising herself into being relatively alright with it.

Adam stood by silently watching her and wondering what she was going to do. She was a fairly stubborn person, and he knew it was pointless trying to reason with her or tell her what to do. By now, he knew that she would have well analysed the situation and would confidently be able to justify every point he could raise in disagreement. Feeling lost and unable to cope or take charge of the situation, he bottled up his feelings and took the coward's way out. He convinced himself that, ultimately, he was only responsible for himself. He rationalised that in any event he was not going to do anything wrong anyway. This meant that he didn't need to get so worked up about it all. He also figured that this reasoning would cover him if there were any negative consequences from whatever she did.

The serpent also stood by hardly daring to breathe as he watched Eve contemplating making that long awaited move. All his efforts were about to pay off. He knew that he would win two times over, because surely Eve would convince Adam to eat of the fruit as well. *Adam can't ever resist her, the weakling*, the serpent thought with disgust. He could not wait to see the look on God's face when he realised what his precious creations had done.

Eve inched forward towards the tree, each step carefully premeditated and measured. Eventually she found herself standing at the foot of the tree, and as she reached out a hand to pluck the ripest fruit on a low-hanging branch, the tension in the air was so thick you could have cut it with a knife.

Time seemed to stand still and Eve appeared to be moving in slow motion. After what seemed like an eternity, she finally plucked the fruit from the branch and held the prize in her hands. She examined the fruit in its entirety, turning it over slowly as she looked at every inch of its luscious surface. She noted that the skin was smooth and that the flesh underneath seemed firm. Eve realised that the fruit was very ripe and that it had a very enticing smell that filled her nostrils with its aroma. It made her hungry for it immediately, and her stomach churned and growled in anticipation.

Again, Eve had the opportunity for any last minute thoughts and doubts to change her mind. Typical of her usual mindset, she chose to ignore whatever she was feeling or thinking. There was no turning back now that she was already committed to the act. Slowly she raised the fruit closer to her eagerly awaiting mouth. By now, she could really smell the strong aroma of the ripe fruit as it wafted up towards her nostrils. Her brain began to receive strong signals that this had to be a good fruit. She felt so sure that anything that smelt as delicious as this could never be bad for you.

Just Want to be Loved for Me...

As Eve bit into the firm skin of the fruit, she was delighted to find that underneath it, the flesh was as delicious as she hoped it would be. As she began to chew on it, the juices were released. It had a sugary sweet taste, and she experienced a range of distinctive flavours as it hit the back of her throat. This was a strange sensation that her palate had never experienced before. She paused after a couple of mouthfuls half expecting to become faint or to drop down dead on the spot. On the contrary, she felt absolutely fine – never better! – and she knew at once that the serpent had been right.

Adam, too, was filled with a wild mix of emotions as he stood there watching her with expectation. He could not bear the thought that she might die as a result of this action, and he certainly did not want to discuss it with anyone. Emotionally he felt torn and numb inside. He breathed out a huge sigh of relief when he realised that after a couple of mouthfuls Eve had not collapsed to the ground. In fact, she appeared to be happier than she had been in a long time and elated that she was the one to have discovered this treasure that lay untapped in their midst.

She called Adam to come over, and with much animation and enthusiasm, she began to tell him all about the forbidden fruit. She encouraged him to try it, and although he resisted at first, it was not long before she was able to persuade him that there was no harm in taking one little bite. In any event, he could not bear to be without her or to displease her in any way except when he was teasing her. In his innate desire to please her, he totally forgot about his loyalty and commitment to the relationship he had with God.

As they both revelled in the discovery of the fruit, laughing and joking about whether they felt any smarter now, the serpent quickly made his excuses and left. He could not wait to be alone so that he could gloat and revel in his victory over God.

He went over the scenario in his mind again and again. He remembered how he had almost given the game away when Eve raised the fruit to her waiting lips. He too had nervously been licking his lips and could almost taste the fruit as Eve bit into it, anticipating the sweet taste of victory. In that decisive moment, he had to restrain himself from letting out a whoop of joy. Luckily, he stopped himself in time and settled for a knowing smile instead. He could not wait for the inevitable events to unfold as a result of what they had done. These humans were so gullible. How could God have placed ***them*** at the pinnacle of his creation? What was he thinking?

The aftermath

Both Adam and Eve were surprised by how normal they felt. They still did not feel sick or faint. They realised with a start that they were not going to physically die as God had told them they would. On the other hand, they also did not feel any smarter than before. They certainly didn't feel like gods, whatever that was supposed to feel like. In fact, they felt exactly the same. Nothing had changed! Was it possible that God had played a trick on all of them, including the serpent? In any event, they had found a new food source that would definitely add variety to their current diet.

It all felt like an anti climax, a feeling much different from what they had been expecting. After such a big build

Just Want to be Loved for Me...

up, they now felt flat and let down. They could not have known that this is exactly how the serpent (Satan) works to trick his victims. He often plies the innocent with half-truths, innuendos and false promises to get them to do his bidding.

Adam and Eve realised that they had already wasted far too much time contemplating the matter. They both had lots of things that needed to be done before the day was over. They returned to work earnestly trying to make up for lost time.

As the day went on, they chatted as they worked as usual. Adam paused for a moment to respond to something that Eve had just said. As he did so, he blinked several times to adjust his eyes. He felt as though he was actually seeing Eve for the first time. He noticed everything about her, from her small beautiful face to her firm upright breasts, her narrow waist and full rounded hips, and her long slender legs. As he looked down the length of her lovely body, he realised she was naked.

He was also shocked to find that he felt uncomfortable and embarrassed seeing her that way. He was at a loss for words and could not understand why he felt this way. He noticed too that Eve's face was also flushed and she seemed ashamed that he was looking her over so intently. It had never bothered her before. Instinctively she moved one arm to cover and protect her breasts and the other to cover her pelvic area. She had been looking at him intently too, taking in the full of extent of his strong male physique. He noticed however that she had turned her head away shyly when she saw the fullness of his manhood. Adam looked down to see what had caused her to turn away, and it was as if he was seeing himself for the first time. He was suddenly aware of the need to cover himself. This feeling of shame was very strange to him, and he was not sure how to deal with it.

They found some large fig leaves to cover themselves. They then settled down in the thick foliage of the trees where they could be safely hidden from God's eyes while they tried to work out what was happening to them. They were both still in shock and wondered if this was what it meant to be 'God like'. If so, they were not sure that they liked it all. They also needed to try to work out what to do and how best to get things back to normal.

Judgement time

As the sun went down and the air began to cool, they heard someone walking in the garden. Instinctively, they both jumped nervously, panic stricken at the thought of being found. They knew it was God because he always came to see them at this time of day. They were usually so glad to see him, and they would drop whatever they were doing to run up and greet him. They always had so much to tell him, and they looked forward to his regular visits. On this ill-fated day, however, they were quiet. When God did not see them coming to greet him, he called out to Adam asking where he was. Adam was deeply afraid to answer, but he was more afraid to ignore God's call.

Adam swallowed hard, his mouth suddenly dry. In a quivering voice, he answered and told God where he was. He also told him that he had hidden from him because he was afraid, and that he knew he was naked. God's heart sank and he immediately knew what that meant. He quickly asked Adam how he knew that he was naked and whether

Just Want to be Loved for Me...

he had eaten of the tree from which he had been expressly commanded not to eat.

For the first time in his life, Adam felt completely out of his depth and was not sure how to respond. Rather than admitting that he had in fact eaten from the tree, he chose to pass the buck to anyone other than him. He did this as a direct response to how guilty he felt about the situation. He loved God like a father and worshipped him as his creator, and he could not bear the thought that God would be angry and disappointed with him. Unconsciously Adam was desperately trying to get himself out of a very sticky situation. So, he laid the responsibility totally at Eve's feet. He told God that the woman 'HE' had blessed him with was responsible for giving him the fruit to eat. Again, we see Adam passing the buck here, but this time he is trying to shift the blame away from himself and towards Eve ***and*** God. After all, if God had not given him ***that*** woman this would never have happened. He did all of this in a bid to deflect the blame away from himself.

Now it was Eve's turn to be in the uncomfortable glare of the spotlight as God asked her what she had done. She kept her response simple and to a minimum. It was clear to her that this was a very serious situation indeed. She had never seen God angry before, and it scared her so much. She could never have imagined him this way. He had always been a loving, caring father to them. He had always adored Eve especially as the jewel of his creation, and in his eyes she could do nothing wrong.

This situation was different, however; God was clearly displeased with her, and it took her completely out of her comfort zone. She could not bear to look God in the eye.

The expression on his face – one of deep disappointment – cut her to the core of her heart because she knew she had put it there. She simply owned up and told him calmly that the serpent had tricked her and that yes, she **had** eaten the fruit. By now, the serpent had joined them, and he looked on sheepishly as he heard Eve squarely put the blame on him.

As soon as the words escaped Eve's lips, silence descended. All three of them waited anxiously to see what God would say in response to what he had just heard. The serpent could barely contain his glee as he watched Adam and Eve standing there pathetically trying to cover themselves up. They had really messed up, and the funny part was that they did not even realise how much.

Only the serpent had come up against God before. He knew that God's intense love, compassion, grace and sense of fair play was easily matched by his sense of righteous anger and vengeance. God certainly did not suffer fools gladly, and the serpent was sure that Adam and Eve were about to find out just how harsh God could be in meting out punishment.

It seemed as if all three of them waited forever while God pondered what he would say to them. They shifted from one foot to another uncomfortably, and took turns pacing back and forth. Their heads were lowered and they studied the ground, intently observing the tiniest things they had never before noticed. Their arms were clasped tightly around their bodies as they unconsciously tried to protect themselves against any incoming assault. Adam and Eve became aware that their heartbeats were quicker and their breathing had become shallow.

Finally, God spoke and dealt with each one of them in turn.

The first one to be dealt with was the serpent. God told him in no uncertain terms that there would be a punishment for what he had done.

From this day forward, the serpent would be cursed with the following fate …

- He would be cursed even more than all the cattle and the beasts of the fields.
- He would crawl on his belly and no longer be able to walk upright.
- Because of having to crawl on his belly, he would eat dust as long as he lived.
- The serpent and Eve would always hate one another.
- Eve's and the serpent's offspring would always hate one another.
- Eve's offspring would crush the serpent's head, and the serpent's offspring would bite their heels.

This judgement would reduce the possible negative effect that the serpent could ever have again over mankind. In terms of being able to walk around proudly and being respected by all, he would be reduced to crawling around on his belly, which would be an immediate sign to everyone that he had been cursed, and they would know why. God also put a newfound hatred between Eve and the serpent to make sure that they would never again join forces to create more mischief. Finally, God put in place a plan B, which I will come back to later.

Eve was the second one to receive a judgement from God.

He told her that …

- She would experience much more pain in pregnancy and childbirth than she ever would have experienced before disobeying God.
- In spite of this, she would still greatly desire her husband.
- She would no longer be an equal partner with her husband, but rather, he would rule over her.

These judgements on Eve were designed to be very strategic. God realised that it was important for Eve to have some kind of covering. This was because in her innocence, Eve had not realised the full extent of the power, influence and authority that was within her, but she had exercised it when she listened to the serpent and followed his suggestion, and also when she got Adam to do the same. As a result, she had changed the course of their lives forever. God knew that this was only the start of more trouble if Eve were left unchecked. She could become very dangerous; she could use her creativity, her powers of influence, and her organisational skills to create much havoc.

The pain she would experience in childbirth would be a constant reminder of the judgement placed upon her. Despite having to endure this pain, she would still greatly desire her husband and would always seek to please him. The last part of God's judgement, where he tells her that she will be ruled by her husband, was designed to place Adam as a

Just Want to be Loved for Me...

covering over her. This would protect her and ensure that her many skills were kept focused on helping him to achieve their life purpose together.

Today we see many examples of women who walk out from under the covering of the man God has placed in their lives. Some of these women have even become famous. William Shakespeare wrote in *The Taming of the Shrew* that 'hell hath no fury like a woman scorned'. This play depicts how fearsome a woman can be, especially when she feels that she has been hard done by and is not in the mood to listen to any form of reason or to hear what anyone has to say about her situation.

A woman has the uncanny ability to assess a situation quickly and decide what needs to be done. When she is driven by strong emotions, she has the innate ability to conjure up all sorts of clever, innovative and imaginative solutions. When these skills are used positively, both she and her partner can attain new levels in fulfilling their purpose. However, as men have found out to their detriment and sorrow, when a woman uses these unique abilities negatively because of hurt or pain, she can be at her most dangerous. Her plans may even have lethal results. Oftentimes these negative results are not intended. However, the voice of reason that would detract her from such action is lost in the overwhelming tide of her conflicting emotions.

First things

Eve was a unique creation and specially loved by God. She was also the first lady of all things, and for that, she should always be revered. She was the first woman to commune with God and to have a one-to-one relationship with him.

She was also God's first daughter, and he must have taken great delight in watching her as she went about her days in the Garden with Adam. She was also the first to break God's heart because of her sin. She also made him hurt the way any father hurts at his child's misbehaviour. Eve definitely knew the infinite love of the almighty Father, and she was also the first woman to feel his wrath in judgement. Eve was the first woman to love a man (Adam) with all her heart, and she was also the first to break that man's heart and cause him harm. For this one mistake, she would always be remembered and blamed for the state of the world we have inherited.

After listening intently to the judgement handed to Eve and the serpent, Adam knew that it was not going to be good news for him. God turned his attention to Adam and reminded him of what he had done: he had listened to his wife and had eaten of the forbidden fruit although he had specifically been told not to.

Because of this, God issued the following judgements to Adam:

- The earth would be cursed to Adam.
- He would have to work hard by the sweat of his brow all his life to make the ground produce enough to eat.
- The ground would also produce weeds and thorns, making his work more difficult, and Adam would have to eat wild plants.
- This would be the case until Adam died and returned to the earth from which he had been created.

Just Want to be Loved for Me...

Adam was so shocked at this harsh judgement that it felt like his heart had just fallen into the pit of his stomach. He was unable to comprehend the severity of what he was hearing. This all felt like a bad dream, or like he was watching it happening to someone else. He was still unable to raise his eyes to look at God. He knew that things had gone too far to recapture the unity they had once shared. He was afraid to see the hurt and disappointment that he had caused. As the reality of God's judgement began to sink in, Adam heard the voice of God speaking to him once again. He realised with dismay that the judgement was not over yet. In fact, the worst was yet to come.

He heard God telling both him and Eve that he would make them some proper clothes using animal skins. This would replace the impractical fig leaves they were now using. Then the final blow came. God announced that because they were now like gods, knowing the difference between good and evil, they would have to leave the Garden. They could ***not*** be trusted in the Garden anymore, as they might be tempted to continue in their disobedience. In fact, they may even decide to eat from the Tree of Life. This would cause them to live forever as humans. The ability to live forever in this way was not in God's plan for their lives.

God therefore needed to make sure that this would never happen. The only way to be certain was to order them to leave the Garden forever. They would have to face the harshness of life on the outside, forever walking away from the protection and covering they had always known.

Paradise lost

Adam and Eve felt abandoned and bereft as they looked around the beautiful Garden one last time before they left. Their steps were slow and laboured and their hearts hung heavy in their chests as they made their way toward the gates that would lead to the outside world and bar them from ever returning to this blissful paradise. They were afraid of what lay ahead of them. They knew that the judgement that had been passed down on them would kick into action straight away as soon as they stepped outside and heard those gates slam shut.

Once they were outside the Garden, Adam and Eve stood hand in hand for a moment, unable to move as they grieved for the things they had lost. Most of all they missed God and longed for their relationship with him to be reconnected. At that point, all they had was each other and the life they would carve out for themselves in this strange new world.

They were shocked and dismayed to see the bleakness of the landscape. Unlike the lush bounty of the Garden of Eden, the ground outside was wild, rocky, and dry. Although the sun shone as brightly as before, there was no order to nature. The trees and plants grew wildly among the thorns and weeds. It would take Adam a long time to sort things out. As he surveyed the ground before him, which stretched out before him as far as his eyes could see, he felt overwhelmed at the thought of how hard he would have to work to tame it and use it to create the food and shelter that he and Eve would need.

For the first time they both realised what dying actually meant. They had mistakenly thought it meant an immediate physical death where they would no longer be alive or breathing anymore. They now knew, without a doubt, what God had meant when he said they would surely die if they ate of the tree of knowledge: He meant that the difficulty of daily life without having perfect communion with him would feel like dying.

They realised now that this death referred to a spiritual death because it deeply affected their spiritual connection with God. They also knew that they had been shamelessly tricked by the serpent, the result of which was that now, both Adam and Eve were truly, spiritually dead, and their close connection to God had been severed permanently.

Once they were on the outside of the garden wall, God sealed it forever and placed angels to guard it at the east side. They held flaming swords that turned in all directions. This would insure that no one would ever be able to come into the Garden of Eden again.

Why does the enemy hate us?

For years, I asked fellow Christians and spiritual leaders that question, and I never got a plausible answer. What I did get was a huge load of philosophical and spiritual answers. Being a very straightforward and relatively simple person, I really wanted the plain version. For example:

- Why did the serpent want Adam and Eve to be cursed?
- Why did he dislike them (and all of mankind) so much?

- Why did the serpent want God to be angry with Adam and Eve?

The serpent's behaviour did not make sense to me, and it defied any logical explanation that I was able to come up with. My limited knowledge did not help matters, and I felt as though there had to be a missing part of the puzzle.

In the Book of Ezekiel chapter 28, from about verse 11 onwards we read about the King of Tyre. The earthly king was called Ithobalus, but the supernatural king of Tyre was Lucifer. The chapter is really a kind of warning for the prince of Tyre. It is made very clear that the Almighty God rules supreme, irrespective of the powers of earthly rulers or how well established their kingdoms might be. They can all be destroyed in an instant if God decides it should be so.

We read that God created Lucifer as an anointed cherub (angel). He was one of God's brightest and most favourite of the angels. He shared a very close relationship with God. This chapter goes on to tell us that he was created perfect in all his ways and was allowed by God to live on the earth and have dominion over it. His main responsibility was to lead the angels in worship on the mountain of God.

Eventually Lucifer's heart began to change. His sense of pride began to overcome his loyalty to God. When he saw that things were going so well on earth, he was certain it was all because of him. He began to question his own subservient role, and he wondered why *he* should be the one to lead the angels in worshipping God. He became so full of his own importance that he forgot about the purpose that God had created him to fulfil.

Just Want to be Loved for Me...

He told himself that he could so easily change things, and then he would be like God. He would be worshipped instead of being 'just' the worship leader. His pride grew steadily as his plan took time to gain momentum. Eventually, he gathered support from a majority of the angels. These weren't just any angels; they were some of the strongest and the most powerful. With them on his side, he was confident that he would win in overtaking God's throne. He led these angels up to heaven to challenge God face to face in a bid to take over his reign and to rule supreme over all of heaven. In order to do this, Lucifer and his angels would throw God out so that he would have to live in the lower parts of the earth. This was the first recorded political coup and was one that could never succeed.

It was true that God had taught them all so much. Because of him, their knowledge and power was awesome. Despite this, however, there was no way they could be a match for him. In fact, it was so foolish and misguided of them to even think that they could overthrow God.

When God found out why Lucifer and his followers were gathered before him with expectant, almost victorious looks on their faces, he became very angry with them. He then judged them and condemned them to die in the lake of fire when the world ended. This was a very serious punishment indeed. He also kicked them out of heaven, and as Lucifer tumbled to the depths below he appeared as a bolt of lightning.

Until the end of the earthly age, they would be able to roam and enjoy the world they loved so much and for which they had been willing to risk incurring the wrath of God.

God also caused the earth to be judged. He flooded it causing all living things to die (this was not the same as the flood in Noah's time). He commanded the sun, moon and stars to stop giving light. This was the dark, desolate world that Lucifer and his followers inherited. They were sentenced to roam around aimlessly until the time came for them to be destroyed when the world ended.

The crime they had all committed was that of wanting to be like God. They had not taken advantage of, enjoyed or appreciated all that God had given them.

Once I read this Biblical account of what had happened to Lucifer, I understood that he and his angels (demons) are always on the lookout for ways to completely and utterly undermine and destroy mankind. There are several reasons why Satan hates us so desperately:

Satan hates us because we are better looking than he is

Lucifer is described as being one of the brightest cherubs. He was handsome and he knew it. Every precious stone was his covering. He was also musically talented, and we are told that the workmanship of his tabrets and pipes was second to none. God was able to show his creativity and the variety of his workmanship by giving Lucifer all of these talents. God was very proud of Lucifer for this reason.

However, much to the annoyance of the fallen angels and Lucifer, when God made man he did something different and very, very special. He made us ***in his own image and likeness***. This means that we not only look like him but we have his character as well. This made the creation of man unique in a way that had never been seen before. Lucifer

Just Want to be Loved for Me...

is completely jealous that God loved us so much that he made us to be mini versions of himself. In spite of how handsome Lucifer was, he had never been given the honour and privilege of being created in God's image.

Although Adam and Eve had not yet realised it, they were built with the ability to do the things that God could do. This was the power contained within their emotional, physical and spiritual make up. It was already within them, ready to manifest itself when God knew the time was right. It is important to realise that this did not make them gods in their own right. It clearly meant that they were very much like GOD, who was their father. They would be able to use their God-given power under God's supreme authority and guidance.

This is confirmed in the book of Psalms chapter 8. In verses 4 and 5 it says, "What is man that you are mindful of him … for you have made him a little lower than Elohim." The word *Elohim* means 'Almighty God'. So this means that we are made just a little lower than God. It is very important that we understand this and realise who we are and the purposes for which we were created.

It is obvious that Lucifer knew he was inferior to Adam and Eve as soon as they were created, and he was furious with God for creating them this way and not him. In fact, he hated them for the very fact that they lived and breathed and were loved by God.

After his fall, Lucifer became known as Satan. The meaning of this name conveyed who he was now. The name Lucifer was no longer appropriate, as it referred to the wonderfully bright, anointed cherub that God had created in the beginning.

Satan hates us because we were given his old job

Once Satan had shown an unwillingness to worship God or to lead the angels in worship, God decided to do something about it. He created Adam and Eve for the sole purpose of worshipping him and being a part of his family. This means in real terms that mankind has Satan's old job. Therefore, he hates us because we are doing the job he once had, even though he did not want it.

Satan hates us because we were given his domain

Although Adam was created in the wild, he was not left there for long. He was brought to the Garden of Eden and given dominion over all the earth, as well as the creatures and plants that filled it. When Eve came along, he happily shared this dominion with her as his wife. God loved them both without question. Unfortunately, what they did not know was that long before their time, the same dominion had been given to Satan. He had lived on earth and had complete charge of it all. This adds to all the anger and hatred that he has for us.

The plan of the enemy

You can well imagine how much Satan hated Adam and Eve when he saw how they had been created in God's image, but along with this hatred, there was the kind of jealousy that comes from too much love and adoration. He admired them because God had created them just like himself, and this was something Satan knew that he would never be. So, as far as Satan was concerned, he would just hatch a plan that would wipe the smile off everyone's face.

Just Want to be Loved for Me...

God had passed judgement on him because he had sinned by not being happy with how God had created him and because he had wanted to be like God. Satan reasoned with himself: *What if I can get these weak humans to make the same mistake I made? What will God do to them? Will he give them special favour, or will their judgement be as harsh as mine was? It will serve God right to see that his perfect little creations are actually no better than I am.*

Satan knew God very well. He knew that God is always good and pure, and that he does not change, even when everything around him does. If Satan's crime was that he wanted to be like God, his punishment was eternal disconnection from God and destruction in the lake of fire when the world ends.

Therefore, Satan had reasoned, *if God is as fair as he says he is ... and he does not change ... then surely, if the humans commit the same crime I committed, they will have to face the same punishment I will face when the world ends.*

Satan did not really care and had no loyalties; after all, he had nothing to lose. Although he was free to do as he wished, he was also very clear about what his future held. He didn't want to be in that lake of fire alone. The more people he could steer onto that path, the better. As the old saying goes, misery loves company.

Many people have long debated what Eve's actual sin was. Many people are convinced that it was the sin of disobedience. This is because she directly broke a commandment that God had given to both her and Adam.

When we read verses 5 and 6 in chapter 1 of Genesis, we learn that the serpent told Eve that she would not die but that her eyes would be opened and she would be like God. The fruit looked good to the eyes for eating ... ***and*** it would supposedly make her wise ('like God').

It is as simple as that. She had committed the same sin that Satan had committed all that time ago. Both she and Adam desired to be God. This was what Satan, in the shape of the serpent, had been after all this time. Now that his mission was accomplished, Satan could not wait to hear what God would say to Adam and Eve when he spoke his judgments upon them.

God was heartbroken because he knew exactly what had happened. As God, he also knew what had to come next. There was no other way out for the man and woman he had so lovingly created. He is a just God, and justice had to prevail. His heart was heavy and it made him very angry indeed. So while the serpent looked on, barely able to conceal his victory, God pronounced his judgement on both Adam and Eve.

The sin they had committed now had the effect of disrupting the connection they'd had in their relationship with God. The eternal consequences of this sin would be passed down from generation to generation through the man's seed until the end of the world finally came.

It also meant that mankind would forever be destined to follow along the same path as Satan and his followers. They too would be free to inherit the earth for as long as they lived. However, when the world ended, they too would be cast into the lake of fire and destroyed. This would finally – eternally – sever any connection with God.

Let's imagine for a moment how the serpent, Satan, would have behaved if God had simply forgiven Adam and Eve and let them off with a mild admonishment. Like a naughty and spoilt child, Satan never would have let it go: 'I always knew that God was not fair and that he loves humans better than all his other creations!'

He never would have let anyone forget how unreliable God was and how incapable he was at sticking to his word. He would have continually accused God of having one rule for him and another for his favourites.

God knew all of this, and as much as it hurt him to do so, he fully stood by his words. God does not change with the wind as humans do, and he does not lie.

Cheekily, this is exactly what Satan had known God would do. He knew that God would have to dish out the same punishment to Adam and Eve if they committed the same sin that he had committed. They too would have to die when the world ended. This was the same punishment that had been given to him and his fallen angels. He was now basking in the ambience of his victory, and he intended to make sure that everyone knew about it.

The Plan 'B'

But the serpent (Satan in disguise) had pushed his luck a little too far. First, he had unsuccessfully attempted to overthrow God completely and to take over as the ultimate ruler, and now he was trying to get the upper hand by interfering in God's plan for mankind and the world.

He seems not to have understood who he was dealing with. He didn't realise that it would take a great deal of stupidity and bravery to go up against the Almighty Creator and God of the known universe and beyond. He was deluded in thinking that he had even the vaguest chance of getting one over on God. It is a foregone conclusion that God will always be the victor in any situation. God is omnipotent and as such, he is all-powerful. Therefore, Satan does not stand a chance against him.

What Satan did not know was that at the same time that God was dispensing out his judgements to all three of them, he was already thinking ahead. He had already prepared a solution to the problem that would result in giving mankind a way out of the predicament they now faced.

If you go back and re-read the judgement issued against the serpent, you will notice that God said he would bring enmity between the serpent (Satan) and the woman for generations to come. God also told the serpent that the woman's offspring would crush his head and that he would only be able to bruise the heel of mankind.

This part of the judgement paved the way for mankind to ultimately get the victory over any plan that Satan or his principalities would try to execute over them. Whilst it is true that evil may 'bruise our heads' or cause discomfort, pain or anguish, ultimately, that wound is destined to be temporary. In other words, evil may win certain battles against us, but it is guaranteed that Satan and his minions will lose the ultimate war. This is because of God's love and mercy towards us, which is demonstrated in the way he prepared a way of redemption for us through his son, Jesus Christ. All we have to do is to reach out and accept him.

In the same way that it was Adam and Eve's choice whether or not to disobey God's express command regarding eating the fruit of the tree, we too have the choice to obey God by not sinning against his word and by accepting Jesus as our Saviour. The redemption he offers has been given to us on a plate and is available to everyone. All we have to do is to reach out and accept it.

The way out

In the Old Testament, we read of sacrifices being made to atone (or make up for) the sins people committed. God gave them certain rules that they were required to follow to make sure that their sacrifices were acceptable to God. One of the main conditions was that in any sacrificial offering to God, the offering should be the first of whatever it was. It should also be of the highest quality and should therefore be perfect and without blemish. This was irrespective of whether the offering was an animal or a grain that had just been harvested.

The most important point to note here is that when we give something to God it should be the best of all that we have. It should not be our leftovers or something that we do not want to keep anyway. This also applies to our tithes, our offerings and our time. They should all be offered to God first, not last, to honour the relationship we have with him.

The Hebrews in Old Testament times would make regular sacrificial offerings to God. Once a year, on a special day called Yom Kippur there would be a communal sacrifice. This was a time of dedicated fasting and prayer for the whole nation. Of the many rituals performed, one is very relevant to us today. Two identical goats / lambs were chosen, and one was sacrificed to God in the usual way. The other had a special red ribbon tied around its horn, and a second red ribbon was placed on the temple door. The priests then prayed all the sins of the people onto the animal, after which it was led away. The red ribbon allowed people to know its purpose so that they would not capture the goat or try to kill it to be eaten.

When the animal had met its death and its blood had been shed, the sins of the people were considered paid for and cleared until the next year when this ritual would be done again. According to the Bible, when the animal died, the red ribbon on the temple doors miraculously turned white, which signified that the debt had been paid.

Despite all the sacrifices the people made, the debt of their sin could never be fully repaid and cleared because of how big it was. No creature was ever going to be worthy to clear the sin debt for all of mankind, and any attempt to do so would only give a temporary reprieve. God knew that it would take a human to clear that debt and wipe the slate clean. This would also provide the eternal re-connection that had been severed after the fall of Adam and Eve.

However, no regular human could ever qualify for such a task. Certainly, there were plenty of first-borns who were physically perfect, meaning they met the requirements of animals that were to be sacrificed. However, they all lacked

Just Want to be Loved for Me...

the essential ingredient – that of being born without sin. All people are born in sin. The effects of Adam's original sin will always be passed down through his seed to every generation. Therefore, no regular human being could ever qualify to become the ultimate sacrifice to atone for all of mankind's sins.

As time went on, there were more and more prophecies in the Old Testament about the promise of a Messiah whose special birth and life would be dedicated to God. He would become the ultimate human sacrifice, and this would be his purpose for coming to earth. Throughout the scriptures, we get a full picture of who he would be. His life was mapped out, from his special birth to the kind of life he would have, as well as his ministry and finally his sacrificial death. The details were meticulously recorded in the scriptures, and they even included specific details about the location and conditions of his actual birth. You can read some of these prophecies in the book of Isaiah chapter 53 and in the book of Psalms chapter 22 where the Messiah's death is described.

As Christians, we know that the Messiah has actually already come in the person of Jesus Christ. He was the perfect example to us all of how to live a life without sin. His death signified the ultimate human sacrifice, and he finally paid the price for Adam and Eve's original sin. Jesus' death on the cross made it possible for all of humanity to finally be free and able to spiritually re-connect with God on a one-to-one level.

Knowing that the price has been paid for our sins, we are able to access the benefits of being sons and daughters of God and to dedicate our lives to him accordingly. All we have to do is to fulfil a few basic criteria.

There is nothing complicated about it. I say that because the following steps have been misrepresented and overcomplicated by many people. In this way, Satan has been able to keep large amounts of people from establishing that crucial link with God because they mistakenly think that they will never be able to commit to what seems like a complicated salvation.

They are therefore losing out on the blessing of walking in God's spirit and are denied access to fulfilling their true destiny and the purpose for which God created them.

True salvation

The following four criteria are the basic steps you need to take to claim your right to salvation and inheritance through Jesus Christ.

1. Believe with all your heart
- That Jesus was the manifestation of God on earth and in the flesh (the Messiah).
- That he came to earth to be an example to us and to die for our sins.
- That because of his death, resurrection, and ascension into heaven, you now have the chance to be saved, to be guided by his Holy Spirit in your daily life (which he gave to us before returning to heaven), and to live with him for eternity in heaven.

Just Want to be Loved for Me...

2. Repent of your sins
- This means being genuinely sorry for your sins and asking God to forgive you and to change your life.
- After you repent of your sins, you then need to make a complete turnaround in the way you think and feel about sin. You must be willing to change your life so that you can live for God.

3. Be baptised in water
- The Greek word *baptiso* is used in the New Testament to denote baptism, and it means to be fully immersed in water. This is what happens when you are baptised and your whole body is covered by the water.
- This is an outward sign to the world that you have decided to change your life by accepting God as your heavenly Father and Jesus as your Saviour.
- Being baptised in water identifies you with the death and burial of Jesus Christ.

At some point, you will also be baptised with the Holy Spirit. He will live within you, and will become your personal guide and supporter as you develop your relationship with God.

4. Begin a relationship with God
- This is done by getting to know him and learning all you can about him.
- You can do this by praying and talking to him, by praising him with singing and clapping your hands, and by giving him your tithes and offerings.

- You should also read the Bible to learn all about His character, specifically the things he likes and dislikes concerning how we should live.

You will also learn about the intents and purposes he had in mind when he created you. Best of all, you will share in knowing His ultimate plans for the world and how they will be manifested during these challenging times in which we live.

Most valuable of all is that you will have God's living Word, the Bible, at your fingertips as a reference guide to help you to live your life the way He intends you to do.

Moving on

By following these simple steps, you can change your course from the negative path you might be on right now. This path is not the one that was intended for you by God, your creator. You inherited it because of the original sin of Adam and Eve.

If you know in your heart that this describes your life, please understand that your current path will only lead to death, destruction and eternal separation from God.

But it doesn't have to be this way! God created you with free will, and you can freely choose to let go and let God step into your life, take you by the hand, and lead you into the destiny for which he created you.

Once you accept Jesus as your personal saviour, your destiny is changed and you step onto a path that leads to

Just Want to be Loved for Me...

eternal life. Again, this opportunity is open to everyone in the whole world.

Sadly, large numbers of people do not know about this, or they have been led to believe that salvation is a complicated and onerous process. They immediately fear that accepting Jesus as their Saviour will require them to become instantly perfect. If you have struggled with this fear, please know that this is **not** the case. You are not required to make any changes by yourself; if you could, then what would you need God for?

You are only required to sincerely open your heart and your life to God, and **he** will lead you to do what he wants you to do.

The God of second chances

Today I want you to be encouraged that no matter what your situation is, it can be turned around. Too often, people are doubtful that they could ever be good enough to become a Christian. They are haunted by both their past and their present. With their own natural eyes they are not able to see how they could ever get out of the situation they are in. The Christians they know seem to be so holy, and they are sure those people would never understand some of the things they have been through. They also feel that they would never be accepted by those Christians.

You may even be in a bad situation that you freely walked into and now you don't know how to get out of it. It is possible that you did not fully realise the negative impact it would have on you or what the ultimate consequences would be. Just like Eve, you could have been naive and too trusting. Now things have gone so far that you do not even know how to walk away. You feel completely trapped.

Take heart

There is always a spiritual way to turn things around. God can show you how to use the power within you to transform your situation from being a curse to being a blessing.

I wanted to end this book with the story of Eve because she is one of the strongest examples in the Bible of a woman who has experienced this very thing. Her actions caused the whole of humanity to inherit a judgement of sin and an eternal disconnection from God. Yet in the moment of issuing her judgement, God's love, mercy and grace provided a way for her to be used to bring about a solution to prevent mankind from eternal spiritual death.

God is truly a God of second chances. In spite of all that Eve had done, He was able to forgive her and turn the situation around. Like Eve, sometimes we fall into carefully laid traps set by the enemy because we are so desperate to find acceptance, love and happiness.

But it's important to remember that Adam and Eve were *like* God, and as such, he would have given them all the power and authority they could handle when the time was right. In following the serpent's lies and persuasion, they were trying to fast track the blessing they would have received anyway. Being typical human beings, they wanted that blessing ***now***, and they were not willing to wait and simply trust what God had told them. This caused them to incur the wrath of God.

Just Want to be Loved for Me...

We see the same thing in the New Testament in the book of Matthew chapter 4. After being baptised by John the Baptist, Jesus is led into the wilderness where he is tempted by Satan. The important thing to note is that after not eating for such a long time (forty days and nights), Jesus was very weak and vulnerable. Satan came along and played on this weakness. He offered Jesus all sorts of rewards if only he would bow down and worship him.

The crazy part of all of this is that Jesus was God in the flesh and as such would eventually possess all that Satan was offering him anyway. Satan was hoping that Jesus could be tempted to fast track the blessing and own all the earthly kingdoms now, and if he did so, he would lose his exalted position as the Son of God as a result. Thankfully, Jesus was way smarter than that and had already seen the bigger picture. He could not be swayed at all and was able to quickly and confidently send Satan on his way.

Eve was given a second chance to make things right. In fact, Jesus, the Messiah, was born to a young woman called Mary. As a daughter of Eve, she was pure; she would therefore not pass down the judgement of sin to her son. In every other case in the Bible, judgements were passed down through the male line. God cleverly used Mary to bring forth the Messiah. The child was spiritually conceived and therefore was not contaminated with the male human seed carrying the sin within it.

Thus, ultimately it was through Eve and her female seed that the sinless Messiah entered the world. It was only in this way that he could become a precious sacrifice without blemish to pay the ultimate price to atone for all our sins.

What an awesome comeback for Eve and her female descendants. Through this example, we see the full glory and omnipotence of the true and living God, and it did not end there. Eve moved on with her life and settled into the routine of living outside of the Garden of Eden.

Later on in her life, Eve encountered problems again when her family became dysfunctional. Her two sons Cain and Abel were constantly at odds with one another. Eventually, Cain killed Abel, and because of this horrific act, he was forced to move away and live far from the family. With one son dead and the other one lost to her forever, Eve cried out to God in her distress. Once again, God was faithful to hear her cries and to answer her prayers. He allowed this special first family to have a second chance to start all over again. He blessed Eve with a new son whom she and Adam called Seth. His birth marked the start of all things new, and they made sure that they took advantage of this second opportunity. They were finally able to move on and to grow their new family. It was from this lineage that the Messiah would eventually come and not from Adam and Eve's first two sons.

Let's think about this for a minute. How would God get the glory if he always used someone holy and pure to carry out his will? Although using very holy people is sometimes necessary to fulfil not only their purpose but God's as well, the greatest glory comes when God is able to use someone considered unworthy to bring about his purposes – someone of no social standing … someone who is not necessarily respected or even well known by others. It is in these examples that the full glory of God is seen. People will know in their hearts that the only way that person is able to do the things they do is because of the power of God working through them.

Just Want to be Loved for Me...

A final word of encouragement

Many modern women have found themselves in Eve's situation. If you're reading this and thinking, *I am one of those women*, take heart: Whoever you are and whatever your situation, God is waiting to give you a second chance to become the very special person he created you to be. He also has a special purpose that only ***you*** are supposed to fulfil whilst you are here on earth. When you are on the correct path, God will fill you with his spirit and you will at last find the true meaning of peace and contentment.

We are told very confidently by the old proverb that 'every cloud has a silver lining'. Don't worry that your past experiences and the pain you've suffered have all been a waste. When you encounter other women who are hurting, those experiences will become invaluable to you as you offer help and support to them. They may be in a situation similar to yours or in a worse situation. They may also feel that there is no way out. You will be able to serve as a role model because you have been where they are, and you not only made it through; you made it *out* of your bad situation and are now walking in the destiny that God planned for you all along. Through you and the example of your life, they will be able to look towards the hope of a brighter future with God at the centre of their lives too.

Remember, it all depends on you. All you have to do is to sincerely open your heart and claim your true inheritance. Follow the steps to salvation as mentioned above. You need only to be open to allow God to work in your life, and then he will do the rest.